# SECRET RIVER

British Library Cataloguing-in-publication data.
A catalogue record for this book is available from the British
Library.
ISBN 0 9526031 2 8

First published in 1998 by Green Branch Press, Kencot Lodge,
Kencot, Lechlade, Gloucestershire GL7 3QX, United Kingdom.
Tel. 01367 860588. Fax 01367 860619.

Typeset by Green Branch Press.


Printed and bound by Severnside Printers Limited, Bridge
House, Upton-upon-Severn, Worcestershire WR8 0HG

Cover picture: "The Leadon" (circa 1880) by Edward Smith (1820-
1893), reproduced by permission of Gloucester City Museum.

# Secret River

## an exploration of the Leadon Valley

### By Roy and Pat Palmer

**Green Branch**

*for our grandchildren,*
*William; Georgia and Angus; Jacob and Ellie*

*Details given in this book were accurate at the*
*time of writing, and have been carefully checked.*
*However, the publisher and authors can accept no*
*responsibility for unforeseen hazards or changes.*

# Contents

GENERAL INTRODUCTION ................................................. 6

ACKNOWLEDGEMENTS ..................................................... 9

Index to Maps ......................................................... 10

Walk 1: ROUND EVESBATCH ............................................. 12

Walk 2: COLLIER'S BRIDGE TO ENGLAND'S BRIDGE ................ 16

Walk 3: BOSBURY TO STAPLOW ........................................ 20

Walk 4: ROUND LEDBURY .............................................. 24

Walk 5: LEDBURY TO GREENWAY ....................................... 28

Walk 6: LEADINGTON TO THE LEADON ................................. 32

Walk 7: DYMOCK TO BROOMS GREEN ................................... 36

Walk 8: DYMOCK TO KETFORD BRIDGE ................................. 40

Walk 9: KETFORD TO PAUNTLEY ....................................... 44

Walk 10: ROUND UPLEADON ............................................ 48

Walk 11: UPLEADON TO MALSWICK MILL .............................. 52

Walk 12: HARTPURY TO RUDFORD ..................................... 56

Walk 13: HARTPURY TO MAISEMORE ................................... 60

Walk 14: HIGHNAM, LASSINGTON AND OVER .......................... 64

WORKS CONSULTED ..................................................... 68

Index ................................................................. 70

# GENERAL INTRODUCTION

The Leadon is not widely known outside its immediate vicinity nor sometimes within. Even the pronunciation ('Ledd'n') can cause problems. The river runs for only thirty miles or so (one third in Herefordshire, two-thirds in Gloucestershire) before reaching its confluence with the mighty Severn. Yet it traverses country which though it has not entirely escaped the prairification of modern agribusiness nevertheless ranges from the pleasant to the breath-takingly beautiful, with woods and hills, hopyards and orchards, fields and pastures. This fertile vale with its rich red soil was the native place of John Masefield and the favourite haunt for some years of the Dymock Poets. Ivor Gurney, too, congratulated himself that the Leadon had 'known me – my step'.

For the Romans the Leadon was a 'noble stream'. The Anglo-Saxons named it *Ledene*, which means 'broad', and is related to the Welsh *llydan*. One stretch of the river – upstream from the Severn to Cut Mill in the parish of Redmarley - served as a boundary between two Anglo-Saxon peoples, the Hwicce to the east and the Magonsaetan to the west. The same division was adopted by the dioceses of Hereford and Worcester when they were set up in the late seventh century. (The see of Gloucester was established only in 1541, after the Reformation).

The first written mention of the Leadon came in 972 when the possessions of the great abbey at Pershore were confirmed by King Edgar. The description of the parish boundary at Acton Beauchamp, close to the river's source, included a section *Of Lam Seathan in Ledene*, then *Of Ledene in Lin Leahe*: 'From the Claypits to the Leadon ... From the Leadon to Flax Lea'. This line runs close to the present Hidelow Farm, and this seems to lend weight to the suggestion that the stream there should be given primacy over several other candidates as the source of the Leadon.

The river appears again in a Redmarley charter of 978, and then just over a century later is often mentioned in the Domesday Book (1086), sometimes in connection with the watermills it powered. In its heyday the river drove over a dozen mills, some with more than one pair of stones, and its feeder streams almost a score more. All this was in the area of 120 square miles drained by the Leadon and its main tributaries, the Preston, Kempley, Glynch, Ell and Tibberton Brooks.

Several of the mills are still intact, though none is currently active. Upleadon Mill worked until 1995, though latterly by electric power.

The headwaters of the Leadon consist of a clutch of small streams flowing from a range of hills on the Worcestershire-Herefordshire border, seven miles roughly north-west of Great Malvern. The river flows south in Herefordshire, skirting Bosbury and Ledbury. Soon after crossing into Gloucestershire, near Dymock, it swings to the south-east and eventually reaches the Severn just short of Gloucester.

In its entire course the Leadon manages to avoid traversing a single town, or even a village of any size, and this makes it seem shy, even secretive. In reality, of course, the settlements have shunned the river, which had a reputation for sudden, catastrophic floods. (In times of heavy rainfall the local sandstone absorbs a great deal of water, then rapidly releases it when saturation point is reached). John Masefield, born in Ledbury in 1878, remembered all his life 'the power and terror' of the 'angry red water' of the Leadon in spate. Over the years great efforts have been made to try to minimise such flooding. Mill dams have been removed, channels deepened, banks raised, trees cut down. Even so, few years pass without a flood somewhere on the river, with certain houses reckoning to have at least three in a season.

Some believe that flood prevention work has spoiled certain stretches of the river. Travers Morgan complained in 1987 of 'a dull, ditch-like character' in places. His remark echoed the comment made half a century earlier by John Haines that at Over the Leadon became 'a dirty ditch'. However, Haines, a Gloucester solicitor, botanist and poet, considered the Leadon elsewhere to be 'a very beautiful little river', especially in springtime with its 'golden gush of daffodils'. When the American, Robert Frost, came to live at Leadington in 1914, he and Haines 'for something like a year ... met and wandered over May Hill, the Leadon Valley, and the ridges of the Cotswolds, hunting flowers together, and talking ceaselessly of poets and poetry'. The two men were particularly interested in the Leadon's flora, including 'beautiful autumn flowers, such as the primrose-leaved mullein, the small teasel, and the spreading bell flower'. Edward Thomas, another of the poetic fraternity which gathered at Dymock, wrote to a friend in 1915: 'You would like the country between Dymock and Redmarley d'Abitot: the red marl, the green grass, the larches and the Leadon, a beautiful stream there among woods'.

A lesser poet ruefully recalled the same river as he lay under fire on a French battlefield in 1944:

> In Leadon stream the trout still roams
> And takes his fat May fly
> But in this dusty Norman field
> The blessed fly is I.

The homely comment reminds one that local people, too, derived great pleasure from the river. Children learned to swim in its waters. Families picnicked on the banks, as they still do. Boys and girls trudged to school on nearby paths and lanes. Adults walked to work, to pub or to church.

The present book explores the river from source to Severn, following public rights of way: footpaths, bridleways and lanes. The routes chosen keep as close as possible to the Leadon, though some stretches are inaccessible because there is no suitable right of way. In two places (one at Pauntley and another near Highleadon) paths lead to and beyond the river but footbridges are wanting, so these have been avoided.

Fourteen circular itineraries have been described, ranging from 1° to 8 miles (and amounting to some 70 miles in total). For the keen walker, one or more walks can easily be amalgamated. Conversely, most of the longer walks can be abbreviated. All the routes were literally passable when we walked them, though one can never absolutely guarantee that a problem might not arise here or there. One or two farmers encountered, it must be said, made it clear that they had little time for walkers; others – probably the great majority – were pleasant and helpful.

Each of the itineraries is preceded by an introduction covering matters such as archaeology, buildings, history, natural features, traditions, literary associations, and traces of the canal and railway which once threaded their way through the Leadon Valley. There may be a danger in writing about secret places that as a result their peace might be disturbed, their spell broken. Yet it would be miserly not to share the riches of the Leadon with the careful and discriminating visitor.

# ACKNOWLEDGEMENTS

For advice and assistance we should like to thank these people and organisations:

Mrs D. Ballinger, Chris Beard, Ben Bendall, David Bick, Roger Clarke, Phyllis Davies, Barbara Davis, Mrs E. J. Daykin, George Ellis, Penny Ely, Tim England, Mrs Mary Estop, John George, Gloucestershire County Council (Archaeology, Libraries and Rights of Way Departments), Gloucestershire County Record Office, Gloucestershire Wildlife Trust, Prim Goldring, Sheila Green, Linda Hart, Nigel Hayes, Hereford City Library, Herefordshire Record Office, Hereford and Worcester County Council (Rights of Way Department), Mr. D. James Jones, Mr. Bill Kraswall, Mrs. K. J. Kinch, Mark Kitchen (Gloucestershire County Plant Recorder), Mrs. H. Lee-Partridge, W. H. Masefield, John Moakes, National Trust, Miss Zoë Nelmes, Miss E. Okell, Penny Oliver, Lynn Parker, Jack Parry, Mr and Mrs Robert Ross, Mr. & Mrs. H. Thompson, Roger Wade and Michael Woodbridge.

For permission to reproduce illustrations we should like to thank (numbers in brackets are those of Walks):

Archaeology Service, Gloucestershire County Council: photograph of skeleton (8); Mrs M. Estop: photographs by the late Andrew Compton of weir at Durbridge (9), Payford Mill machinery and Hartpury Mill (12); Gloucestershire Record Office: detail from map of Farm Mill, DC/5114 (7) and photograph of footbridge and ford at Ketford, GPS 125/1 (8); Mr John Moakes: photograph of Payford Mill by V. Pollet; Miss Zoë Nelmes: photographs of picnic by Leadon and bathing in Leadon (13); Palmer Collection of Postcards: Leadon at Bosbury (3), street scenes at Ledbury (4), mill and pool at Upleadon (10), Barber's Bridge Station and obelisk (12) and Lassington Oak (14); Mr H. Thompson: photograph of otter hunt (8).

Unless otherwise indicated, colour photographs are by Pat Palmer.

# Index to Maps

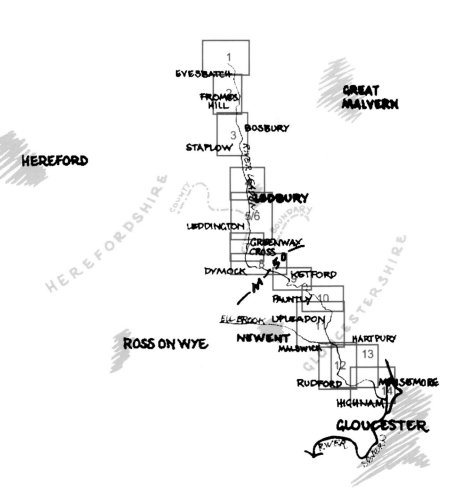

# The Walks

# Walk 1: ROUND EVESBATCH

William the Conqueror's Domesday Book, compiled at Gloucester in 1086, provides the first written record of Evesbatch, as *Sbech*. In 1243 *Esebach* turned up, and apparently this was the local pronunciation until early in the twentieth century. The spelling, *Evesbatch*, had to wait until 1757 for its first appearance, which was on a tombstone at Bromsberrow. The word means 'Esa's stream valley', which takes us back before the Norman Conquest, since Esa was a Saxon name.

ing tower-like structures which were once hop kilns. It has striking red earth, and in due season a wealth of wild flowers. Its breezy uplands afford fine views of the Shropshire Hills, of Bromyard Downs, and of the Malverns.

Unfortunately, the parish is short of footpaths. Plenty are shown on early maps but they were omitted from the definitive record which applies today. However, by walking up from Halmonds Frome and then follow-

*Looking down the Leadon Valley from Evesbatch Church*

One wonders whether Esa's stream might not have been the original name for the River Leadon, which rises above the village. Evesbatch is a place of woods and orchards, fields and hopyards, with several houses hav-

ing a rough quadrilateral of roads (for the most part pleasantly traffic-free), one can circumnavigate the expanse of slopes whose springs and streams combine to form and feed the infant River Leadon. Acton Cross, which is on the itinerary, once had a black-smith called Hodges who re-married with somewhat indecent haste after the death of his first wife. As a result she took to appearing by night at her two children's bedsides and had to be exorcised by the Acton Beauchamp parson and eleven of his colleagues.

Towards the end of the walk, on the right as the road nears Evesbatch, is the 550 foot Ward Hill. A field there called The Bloody Verlands [? Furlongs] may have been the site of a Civil War skirmish between royalists garrisoned at Canon Frome and parliamentary troops from Bosbury. At Evesbatch St Andrew's Church with its tiny wooden bell-turret is well worth a visit. Although the restoration of 1877 amounted more or less to a complete rebuilding, the simple interior has a quiet dignity. One interesting feature is the ancient round font with its decorative Jacobean cover. Another, at the south side of the west end, is the sculpture of a woman clasping a baby. This was Margaret Dobyns, who died in 1658 while attempting to give birth to a son, who also died. Perhaps she lived at the house called Dobyns, which is on our route. Certainly, many former inhabitants of houses and farms seen on the walk lie in the little churchyard; and

*Margaret Dobyns and child*

in the visitors' book at the church there are messages from people once resident who have been drawn back, sometimes from great distances, to see Esa's peaceful valley.

# Walk 1: EVESBATCH

5¾ miles (3 hours), starting at Halmonds Frome (map ref. 675481), with parking on wide grass verge above Majors Arms; or 4¼ miles, starting at Evesbatch (map ref. 685481), with parking on roadside near church.

A. Walk down Snail's Bank (as it is called) past the Majors Arms, then turn right to follow signed path uphill through wood (The Grove), keeping roughly parallel with boundary on left. As slope levels, follow waymarks to right to reach top righthand corner of wood. Cross stile into field with view of Malverns beyond, and go down slope with hedge on left. Cross stile into next field, continuing on same heading. (Evesbatch Coppice, marked to left on O.S. map, has now gone). At bottom, cross stile to reach track. Turn right, and then immediately left over stream, and uphill, past house on right (Old Rectory) to T-junction at Evesbatch by another house (Bauhinia). *This is the alternative starting point.*

*Orchard at Orchard Cottage, Evesbatch*

B. Turn right on road and follow it as it curves left and downhill, passing Evesbatch Court and Church on the left, then orchards on both sides. Reach bridge over River Leadon at bottom. Beyond it, turn left past telephone box. After passing Pound Cottage on the right the road (Hook Lane) climbs, with views to the left of The Farm, with the river below it, and of Pool Farm. Soon after a hopyard on the right, a bridleway sign on the left points uphill to Copley Farm, three fields away. This route, which would cut off a corner, is obstructed at one point, but can be followed by the determined. Otherwise, continue uphill on road, passing Lane Cottage, and at T-junction turn left (signed Bromyard).

C. Follow this road for about 1/2 mile to Acton Cross, passing on the left Copley Farm (where the bridleway emerges) and the track leading to Hidelow Farm (and beyond it, though not accessible to the public, the probable source of the Leadon). At Acton Cross, turn left (signed Bishops Frome). (On the right of this road, after about 100 yards, a willow-framed pool is another possible source of the river). Continue for about 1/2 mile, then turn left (signed Evesbatch). After a further mile, having passed Sinton's End and Kidleys Farm, turn left again (still signed Evesbatch). Stay on this road (Green Lane) for 3/4 mile, passing Ward Hill on right, then Orchard Cottage and Dobyns on the left, to reach right turn (point B.) which leads back to Halmonds Frome and the starting point.

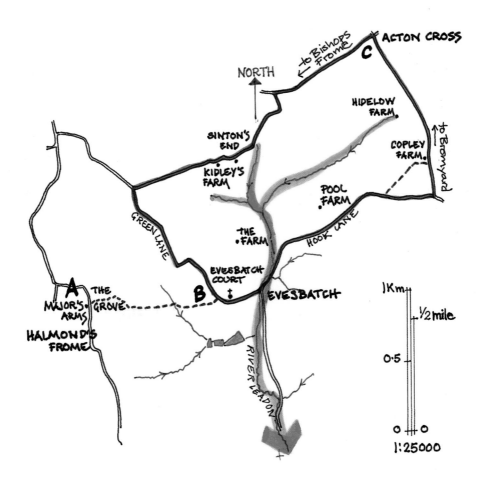

Map: Pathfinder 1018, *Great Malvern*.
Refreshments: Majors Arms, Halmonds
Frome (01531 640371); restricted
opening hours.

*Approaching Collier's Bridge*

Two miles from its source, swelled by a size-able tributary, Steen's Brook, the Leadon flows in a broad and remarkably beautiful valley, flanked by sweeping slopes and wooded hills. From the start of the walk there are fine views of the Malvern Hills and, later, of the distant May Hill. The power of the water was already great enough here to drive the first of its many mills, Dodd's Mill, otherwise known as Bosbury Upper Mill. Thirty years ago the half-timbered house and sandstone outbuild-ings stood derelict. Now they have become an attractive dwelling, hard by the river. The valley is studded with handsome farms, some

still in production, others – such as Bentley's – now purely residential.

The secluded Collier's Bridge stands near a crossing of tracks running east-west from Mathon to Fromes Hill and north-east from Evesbatch to Bosbury. Perhaps Collier was the builder of the bridge, though it is possi-ble the name came from charcoal burners working in Beacon Hill woods. England's Bridge, first recorded in 1831, is equally mys-terious. Again, the name could have come from the constructor of the double-arched bridge with its sturdy cut-waters; or it just might commemorate some distant incursion by the Welsh and resistance from the people of Bosbury. An inn called England's Gate once stood nearby. Catley Cross, a short dis-tance away, provides an insight into a once fiercer landscape: Catley means 'wild cat wood'. Such echoes of the past will not pre-vent the walker from enjoying the tranquil paths and lanes of a particularly beautiful stretch of the River Leadon.

A curious connection with the wider world occurs just off the route, a mile west of Notehouse Farm, at Hill Farm, where in 1840 a Mormon missionary from America, Wilford Woodruff, set about baptising converts in a pond. Over a period of ten years some 2,000 people, including the local policeman, parish clerk and churchwarden, passed through the pond, and many of them emigrated to America. Large numbers of their co-religionists cross the Atlantic in the reverse direction each year to visit Hill Farm – and perhaps the Leadon Valley.

*Leadon Valley south of Collier's Bridge*

*England's Bridge*

# Walk 2: COLLIER'S BRIDGE TO ENGLAND'S BRIDGE
5 miles (2 1/2 hours), starting in section of old road off A4103 just east of summit of Fromes Hill (map ref. 684465).

A. At bend in old road go through gate with both bridleway and footpath signs. Follow bridleway left across field to pass through gate just to left of barn of Spon End Farm. In next field follow track to left downhill to gate at lowest point. Beyond, turn right and follow hedge and brook through further gate. After that, when the brook goes underground continue with old hedge-line on right. At bottom righthand corner of field go right for 75 yards along sunken track to metal gate. Cross next field slightly to left to another gate which gives access to Collier's Bridge.

B. Cross bridge and turn right to gate. Ignoring bridleway sign pointing left, follow grassy track ahead (reputedly a Roman road) with River Leadon on right. Continue through two more gates (the second in a dip), then up a rise and swing right to a third. Go through. (Even though the track may look like a private drive it is a right of way. The wooded Beacon Hill is on the left; Millcroft Cottage and Dodd's Mill are below the track on the right). Keep on the track to its junction with a metalled road. Turn right, then just before the road bridge over the river, cross stile to take marked footpath on left. Follow river bank down big field. *Footbridge on right some two-thirds of the way down provides one possibility for a shortcut.* In bottom righthand corner of field cross stile into orchard, with Bentley's Farm on left. In orchard (called Long Acre) continue on previous heading, over stile in fence, and on to further stile in hedge on far righthand side. Go ahead in field beyond, and when hedge veers to right cross to double stile and footbridge in hedge on far side. In next field follow river bank to stile in hedge to road by England's Bridge.

C. Turn right over bridge and follow road for some 200 yards. Immediately past Catley Cross Farm go over footbridge and stile on right. In field, head slightly to left to reach farthest corner, by clump of willow trees. Cross footbridge and stile in tall hawthorn hedge. Go slightly left with stream on right to field boundary, then across corner of next field to footbridge over Catley Brook. Then go to stile by big oak in righthand corner of next field. Beyond it, turn left and follow hedge past a house (the hamlet is known as The Gardens). Ignore gate on left, and at the back of a second house go over footbridge and stile. Climb slope of field beyond, following lefthand hedge to a stile which leads to road.

D. Turn right and follow road for about 400 yards. At junction turn left up slope, then take signed footpath on right, opposite Notehouse Farm. Follow track down field slightly left to gate. In next field gradually converge on hedge on left, then follow it. (Woodlow Farm is above on left; the River Leadon, Dodd's Mill and Millcroft Cottage below on right). Go through gate in far lefthand corner of field and follow lefthand hedge downhill, ignoring stile on left. At bottom of field go through gap in hedge and cross stream. Beyond, go slightly left along slope towards metal gate. Do not go through gate, but continue with hedge on left to far corner of field. Cross stile on left and go up field with hedge on right. Stay on this heading, always with hedge on right, through a series of fields, via one stile and three gates. Pass through yard of Woodcroft Farm by three more gates, with Dutch barn on right. Keep on track beyond for about 100 yards, then cross stile by gate on right. Continue with hedge on right, passing through two gates, to reach Spon End Farm. Go through yard by stile and two more gates. Follow track through field to return to starting point.

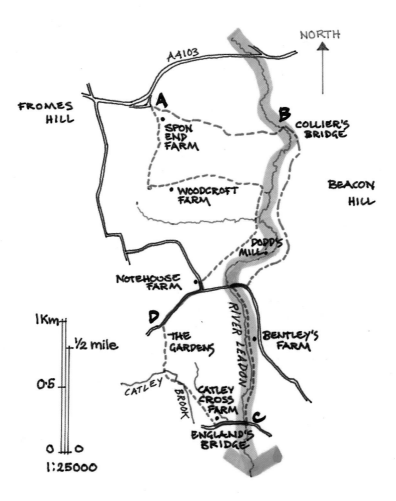

Maps: Pathfinder 1018, *Great Malvern*.
Refreshments: Wheatsheaf Inn, Fromes
Hill (01531 640888). There is also a
transport café at Fromes Hill.

# Walk 3: BOSBURY TO STAPLOW

Bosbury is a quiet place, and its history seems to have been largely uneventful. The Saxons were here, and the name means 'Bosa's fort', Bosa possibly being the scribe mentioned in a charter of 833 as serving King Witlaf of Mercia. The Saxon bishops of Hereford and their Norman successors had a palace at Bosbury. Its great thirteenth century gateway still stands as part of Old Court Farm to the north-east of the churchyard. The detached church tower, one of seven such in Herefordshire, also dates from the thirteenth century. Its massive walls show that the builders had defence in mind, possibly against the Welsh. A story concerning

been engraved on the orders of the vicar as part of a bargain struck with parliamentary soldiers who wanted to pull down the cross as a symbol of popery. The incident forms part of a lively historical novel, *In Spite of All*, by Emily Lyall (Ada Edna Bayley), who often visited Bosbury when her brother was vicar. She died in 1903, and her ashes were buried by a memorial close to the churchyard cross. Though she is now read very little, in her day she was a best-selling writer, as well as being a passionate social reformer. Gladstone admired her work, and one of her novels was read to Ruskin as he lay on his death-bed. The fine church is full of interesting things,

*The Leadon at Bosbury*

including monuments to the Harfords, who also supply some of the central characters in *In Spite of All*. Their sixteenth century mansion still exists at the west end of Bosbury, close to the River Leadon. A suggestion that Prince Rupert slept there during the Civil War is without substance; it was concocted in 1902

the churchyard cross dates from the Civil War of the seventeenth century. The inscription, 'Honour not the + but honour God for Christ', still just discernible, is said to have

purely for the publicity.

Hops are much in evidence near this stretch of the Leadon; Herefordshire now produces more of them than any other English county. Mr Jack Parry, now of Ledbury, formerly ran one of the biggest hop farms in the west of England at Prior's Court, Staplow. (The house has no ecclesiastical connection; its earlier name of Wellington Court was changed by an owner called Prior). The hop pickers were mainly either gypsies or people from Dudley in the Black Country or Abertillery in Wales. Mr Parry remembers that when a gypsy king known as Black Harry died at Prior's Court his magnificent caravan was ritually burned. On a different occasion a fire-and-brimstone preacher who came to harangue the Welsh was run out of the place by exasperated pickers. The Tewkesbury writer, John Moore, spent a considerable time at the Court while doing research for his charming novel of hop-picking, *September Moon* (1957). Mr Parry recalls frequent Leadon floods. In one especially trying year waters rose three times through the flagstones of the floor before completely surrounding the Court. On the credit side, he observed kingfishers, dippers, ring ousels, herons, and even (some forty years ago) corncrakes. He saw the Wye Valley Otter Hunt, but no otters, the last locally having been killed in the 1930s. Five or ten years before that the mill at Prior's Court ceased work. The building is now gone, though a sombre tale survives. It seems that an insanely jealous miller murdered his daughter's lover and disposed of the body. The daughter never learned his fate. She grieved throughout her life and continued to look for him, even after her death. Mr Parry put the story into verses which end with these lines:

*Waggon tunnel beneath canal embankment*

So now when dark, and bats take flight,
She searches in the dead of night,
But should you see her ghostly form -
Face deathly white and quite forlorn -
Remember her, this lovesick maid;
Pass on your way, be not afraid.

Behind Prior's Court runs an imposing embankment (built in 1840), a quarter of a mile long and up to thirty feet high, which carried the Gloucester to Hereford canal over the Leadon. The river still flows through its aqueduct, and the embankment is also pierced by a lofty tunnel which allowed the old-fashioned farm waggons to pass fully-laden. The canal, opened as far as Hereford in 1845, was abandoned only forty years later, its traffic taken over by the railways. (See also Walks 4 and 5).

## Walk 3: BOSBURY TO STAPLOW
5 miles (2 1/2 hours), starting at Bosbury, with parking in village street by church (map ref. 696434).

A. Go south, down track between Bell Inn and telephone box. After passing school playing field, turn left through gap in hedge into hopyard opposite Severn Trent treatment works. Inside hopyard, follow righthand hedge to bottom corner. Go through gap in hedge and over ditch into orchard. Follow fence on right but where it veers off continue on original line. When orchard trees end turn back to left at acute angle to reach stile in hedge to lane by telegraph pole.

B. Turn right down lane. *After group of houses on left (Lower Southfield) a gap in hedge on right gives access to a path – marked X-X on sketch map – which abbreviates walk for any so wishing.* Continue on lane past hopyards and two houses (Hawthorns and Dormers) on right, to junction. Turn right. Go over stream (Coddington Brook, which joins the Leadon immediately to the north of old canal embankment) and up slope to further junction, by the fourteenth century Peg's Farm. Turn right, down Hollow Lane, and pass The Fishery (which preserves a stretch of the former canal) on the left, and Prior's Court on the right. Cross the Leadon and after a second, smaller bridge, go through kissing gate on right. Cross field obliquely to left, following fence and new hedge. (Old canal embankment visible to right). Towards far side of field, turn left (way-marked) and make for rough stile at edge of copse. Over stile, go up slope, veering to right, to reach further stile. Over this, go left through orchard and garden, then along drive of house (The Cottage)

*Hopyard near Bosbury*

to reach road (B4214).

C. Turn right (taking great care, since this road can be very busy). Pass (or not, as the case may be) the Oak Inn on the left and then a house (The Old Wharf – shades of the canal again, which passed beneath the road at this point) on the right. Some 50 yards on a gap in the orchard hedge on the right reveals a stile. Cross field to gated bridge over stream (Stony Brook, where short-cut rejoins route), then veer slightly to right to reach a stile leading to an orchard. Over, continue on original heading, keeping to left of farm buildings (including old-fashioned brick privy) to reach access road to farm (called The Farm). (From this point, the marked route over the next few stiles differs from that shown on the O.S. map). Cross farm road to stile, then go through field, passing to left of pond. Over next stiles cross narrow neck of an orchard to further stile. Beyond this, go left to reach stile by righthand edge of a wood. Cross next field diagonally to left, aiming for stile in fence visible to right of a white house. Continue on same heading

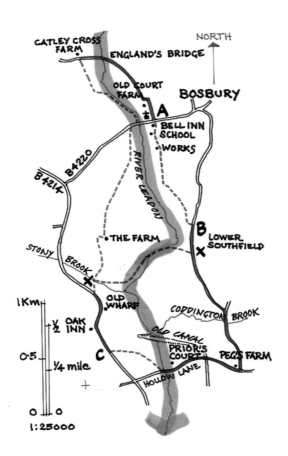

across corner of next field to reach stile on left. After this, follow lefthand boundary by small clump of conifers to further stile. Then cross big field diagonally to far righthand corner, and go over stile to road (B4220) by speed limit sign.

D. Turn right. After 75 yards take signed track on left, alongside River Leadon. Keeping river on right, go through kissing gate, then next field. At the end of this, go through gap in hedge, and then diagonally left across field. Turn right through gate, ignoring stile to left, along track, and reach road by Catley Cross Farm. Turn right, and re-cross river by England's Bridge (for which, see Walk 2). Continue on road, passing hopyards, Old Court Farm and the newly-refurbished village pound, to arrive at the starting point in the village of Bosbury.

Map: Pathfinder 1018, *Great Malvern*. Refreshments: Bell Inn, Bosbury (01531 640285); Oak Inn, Staplow (01531 640621).

# Walk 4: ROUND LEDBURY

The earliest settlement close to Ledbury may be the iron age fort a mile to the west at Wall Hills, where Thomas Blount recorded in 1679 that 'In Ploughing here have been found lately Pike Heads, Arrow heads, Brasse Coynes, Horse Shoes of antic form, and the Bones of men'. The town itself dates from the eighth century, when the first church was established. The name of *Liedeberge*, recorded

*Elizabeth Barrett Browning Institute and Market House, Ledbury*

in the Domesday Book, could mean 'Leoda's fort' or 'fort on the Leadon'. The place-name authority, Eilert Ekwall, albeit with some caution, favours the second of these.

The present church, which Nikolaus Pevsner calls 'the premier parish church in Herefordshire', was built mainly in about 1230, its detached tower paralleling Bosbury's. The quality of the structure is matched by the interest of the many monuments it contains. These include a brass to John Hayward (died 1614) of Prior's Court (see Walk 3), and the effigies of Edward Skynner (died 1631), his extravagantly-hatted

wife, and their eleven children, one of whom (between the couple) is reputed to have been killed by the last wolf in these parts. 'With its golden bird still sailing air', as Masefield put it, atop the spire, the church dominates a handsome town richly endowed with fine buildings. St Katherine's Chapel dates from the early fourteenth century, the Old Grammar School (now a heritage centre), the Feathers Hotel and the Talbot Hotel from the sixteenth. Wall paintings of 1560 came to light in the town council's office at No. 1, Church Lane, as recently as 1988.

The nearby Market House was in existence, though unfinished, in April 1645 when the battle of Ledbury took place. A parliamentary force from Gloucester encamped in the town, led by Colonel Massey, was attacked at dawn by royalists under Prince Rupert, who had marched overnight from Leominster. A fierce running battle developed in the Homend, the High Street and the Southend, as the parliament men withdrew towards Gloucester. The sword of a parliamentary officer fatally wounded in the clash is preserved in the chapter house of the parish church. Prince Rupert lodged for a time at Ledbury Park, then called New House. A subsequent Civil War skirmish is commemorated by a plaque on the Talbot Hotel in New

Street. Across the way from the Market House is the Barrett Browning Memorial Institute, now used as a library. The building may be 'really terrible', as Pevsner puts it, but at least it marks Elizabeth Barrett's connection with the town: from 1809 until 1832 she lived just a few miles away at Hope End, and began writing there. Despite being born in Ledbury (in 1878), John Masefield has no visible memorial. The long narrative poem, *The Everlasting Mercy*, which made him famous if not notorious on its first publication in 1911, drew upon his knowledge of Ledbury low life, and might be called the *Under Milk Wood* of its day. A good deal of the action takes place in the Lion, which Masefield claimed was 'an imaginary tavern' just north of the Market House. It has been suggested, though, that he had in mind the Seven Stars Inn, which not only bears one of the names of the Leo constellation, but is in fact just north of the Market House. Another of Masefield's long narratives is *The Widow in the Bye Street* (1912). The poem may be largely fictional but 'the widow's house' was pointed out in the Bye Street until the 1950s, when it was knocked down with others to make way for the present fire station. The widow's son, hanged for murdering his rival in love, was, wrote Masefield, 'supposed to be a worker on the railway line

*Memorial brass of 1614 in Ledbury Church: John Hayward of Prior's Court, Staplow*

laid towards Newent in my childhood'.

The line, from Gloucester to Ledbury via Newent, superseded a canal constructed in the late eighteenth century, and adopted much of its route. The railway in turn has been closed for over thirty years, though the Hereford-Worcester line through Ledbury, with its magnificent viaduct of 1861 which spans the Leadon Valley, remains in use. Although the canal closed when he was only seven, Masefield remembered all his life the boat people who sometimes invited him aboard to see their neat cabins. The romance of sailing stayed with him, as did a fascination with water, which he saw first in canal pounds, in the mill-race at New Mills, and in the River Leadon. The river bridge, then with a plaque threatening anyone who should damage it with seven years' penal transportation, was only half a mile from The Knapp, where Masefield lived as a child. He would go down after heavy rain to see the drowned fields and the angry red water, and to sense the power and terror of the flood. The New Mills - working until about 1960 - have now given their name to a large housing estate, separated from the river by a new by-pass.

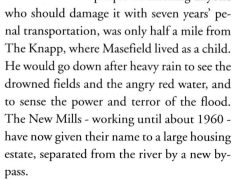

# Walk 4: ROUND LEDBURY

3 1/2 miles (1 3/4 hours), starting in picnic and parking area signed Leadon Valley (map. ref. 702367) by roundabout on A449 near Full Pitcher Hotel, Ledbury.

A.  Go to River Leadon, hidden behind trees, and turn right along the bank, upstream. (This is not an official footpath but the land is owned by the county council, and walking is encouraged. Comfrey, cow parsley and hogweed grow in abundance, together with the less welcome Japanese knotweed). At the bridge, go up bank, cross Little Marcle Road, and continue beyond with river on left. After 1/4 mile cross river (the course of which has been altered here to accommodate new by-pass) by footbridge on left. Go over stile in fence and turn right, with river now on right (and Wall

of the bridge here was the one known to John Masefield). Continue to the roundabout. (The bridge just before it spans what was the leat from New Mills).

B.  Follow road beyond roundabout, signed Bromyard, using lefthand pavement. Pass beneath railway bridge. (This is the skew bridge of 1881. Just before it, an arch can be seen in the embankment on the left. It was through this that the former canal passed beneath the Worcester-Hereford railway line). Beyond skew bridge, turn left at junction (signed Bromyard and Bosbury) on to B4214. Go under bridge, then immediately cross stile on right and follow footpath L 19 with railway embankment on right up three fields, and over successive stiles. At top righthand corner of third field cross stile to track. Go right, passing above tunnel mouth. At staggered crossroads go up steps in bank and follow footpath along bottom of Dog Hill Wood. Keep on path, following signs to Town Centre and ignoring side turnings.

*Talbot Hotel and New Street, Ledbury*

Hills on left), to follow footpath LR 11 (passing farm gate on right) to double stile. Cross big field beyond, aiming to left of viaduct and slightly to right of group of three oak trees. Go through gap in fence and turn right along track towards railway viaduct. At road (A438) turn right and re-cross River Leadon. (A forerunner

Go down broad flight of steps (in Green Lane, part of the ancient road from Hereford to Worcester). Join road, continuing in same direction, and after 80 yards take narrow path beside brick wall on left, leading to churchyard. There, turn right to Church Lane, and at the bottom of this reach High Street by the

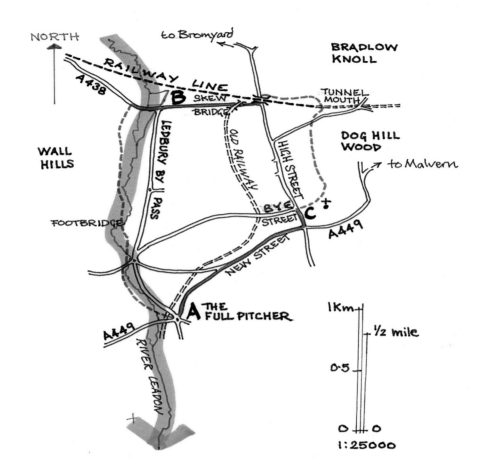

Market House.

C. Turn left. At second set of traffic lights, turn right into New Street (which was laid out before 1232). Pass the Talbot Hotel on the left and continue downhill for about 3/4 mile to reach traffic island by Full Pitcher, and starting point.

Map: Pathfinder 1041, *Ledbury and Much Marcle*. Refreshments: There are several cafés in Ledbury and a dozen public houses, of which those mentioned here are: Feathers Hotel (01531 632494); Full Pitcher Hotel (01531 632688); Seven Stars Inn (01531 632834); and Talbot Hotel (01531 632963).

# Walk 5: LEDBURY TO GREENWAY

South of Ledbury the Leadon Valley widens. Fertile fields sweep up towards Leadington in the west and Donnington in the east. Leadington, in Gloucestershire, is first recorded in the early thirteenth century as *Ledinton*, meaning 'farmstead near the Leadon'. Donnington, across the river in

*Old Nailshop, with Greenway Bridge beyond*

Herefordshire, appears in Domesday as *Dunninctune*, 'the estate associated with Dunna' – a Saxon personal name so widespread that it has given rise to over a score of Donningtons in different parts of England. Hereabouts, one county slips imperceptibly into the next, with the river itself constituting the boundary at one stage. 'This borderland' wrote R. P. Beckinsale in 1939, 'is a rich red soil when the plough has turned it, a blaze of yellow in daffodil time, a mass of fruit blossom in the spring, a reek of cider in the fall, and

pigs and poultry all the year'. All these things are still true, though except for the colour of the soil they are much attenuated from changes in farming practice.

Just south of Ledbury, the historic Hazle Farm, mentioned in Domesday, can boast a distinguished list of owners or occupiers, including the bishops of Hereford, King Harold, the Pauncefoots, the Walwyns and the Eltons. In the early eighteenth century it was bought by Jacob Tonson, the London publisher of Addison, Congreve, Dryden, Milton and Pope. When he took possession, in 1720, he had a survey done of the estate, a beautiful piece of work which is preserved in the Herefordshire Record Office. Tonson died in 1736.

In these parts, literary associations are seldom far away. Several houses in Leadington and one in Greenway were occupied for varying periods by members of a group of friends known as the Dymock Poets. *(Parts of Walks 5 and 7 coincide with stretches of Poets' Paths I and II, eight-mile itineraries which are available locally).* The American poet, Robert

Frost, stayed with his family at Little Iddens for several months in 1914. John Haines, the Gloucester solicitor, botanist and poet, met him 'in one of the flowery country lanes north of Dymock'. They became firm friends, and 'for something like a year', wrote Haines, 'we wandered over May Hill, the Leadon Valley, and the slopes of the Cotswolds, hunting flowers together, and talking ceaselessly of poets and poetry'. Edward Thomas, spending August 1914 at Oldfields in Leadington, walked over three fields 'two or three times a day' to meet Frost at Little Iddens, the 'little house of whitened bricks and black timbers'.

Eleanor Farjeon lodged for part of the same month at Glyn Iddens, where her hosts invited Frost and Thomas, Lascelles Abercrombie and Wilfrid Gibson for supper, and on their home-produced cider inadvertently made 'two brace of poets' if not drunk, then very unsteady. Gibson was living, as he did for several years, at the Old Nail Shop, Greenway, whose 'bird-haunted eaves of thatch', 'black timbers and rosy brick' featured in his verse.

*Donnington Church*

John Masefield was not one of the Dymock Poets, though he knew the area well. In his youth the Pie's Nest, now a private dwelling just off the Gloucester road (A 417) not far from Donnington, was a public house displaying this notice: 'My house is secure, my accommodation good./ Please to step in and taste my home-brewed'. Rather more significantly, the eponymous daffodil fields of Masefield's own poem were at the nearby Hall House Farm, together with a tributary stream of the Leadon of which he wrote: 'Its passage through the Hall House Meadows gave me at all times the liveliest delight. When I came upon the story of *The Daffodil Fields* in a foot-note to an old book on Iceland, I resolved to tell the tale in verse, as happening in three more or less imaginary farms along the course of the brook'.

# Walk 5: LEDBURY TO GREENWAY

## Itinerary: 7 1/2 to 8 miles (3 1/2 to 4 hours), starting as in Walk 4.

A. Turn right out of the picnic area and walk away from the roundabout along the Ross Road (A 449) over the River Leadon, passing sports fields on the right. Turn left along lane signed Leadington 1 1/2. (Tree-lined course of river, Hazle Farm and a later house on site of Hazle Mill can be seen to left). Follow lane as it swings sharply to right by drive to Siddington Farm (meaning farm at south of estate) and continue uphill, passing Orlham Farm (the name means alder field) on the right. At the junction of roads by a letter box, turn left (and in so doing, cross from Herefordshire into Gloucestershire).

B. After 300 yards ignore footpath signs to left and right (unless choosing to include Walk 6 as a detour from this point). Continue on lane, passing a series of historic houses and farms, including Glyn Iddens and Little Iddens on the right, and Henberrow, Mirabels, Haytraps and Swords on the left. Eventually, 1 1/2 miles after turning left by letter box, turn left again (signed Brooms Green, Bromsberrow, Ledbury) by Drews Farm, and pass Greenway House and the drive to the moated Bellamys Farm on the left. Cross the former canal and railway bridge, and then Greenway Bridge over the River Leadon. Beyond that, reach Greenway Cross, with the Old Nail Shop on the left.

C. Cross the road (B4216), and take lane signed Brooms Green and Bromsberrow. After just over ° mile turn left (crossing back from Gloucestershire into Herefordshire) along track at edge wood indicated by footpath sign next to house called Upper Lodge. (A detour of a few hundred yards along the lane at this point leads to the Horseshoe Inn). After the second of two gates, leave track and follow fence on left. When fence turns away to left, keep on original line to reach stile in fence ahead. Go straight across field in direction shown by signpost and waymark, roughly parallel with lefthand boundary, and aiming to right of complex of buildings (Donnington Farm). On far side of field go over stile by gate, then cross bridge over brook which feeds lake on left. In next field, follow lefthand hedge for 100 yards, then turn left through hedge and take stile to field beyond. Turn right, towards Donnington Church. Go through churchyard by two gates, and cross meadow beyond to reach lane by third gate.

D. Turn right along lane. Where lane bends sharply to right, turn left at no through road sign. By drive to The Nurdens go through ornamental metal gate on right. Cross field obliquely to left, aiming to right of two big grey barns seen in distance. Go over stile in hedge. Beyond, on path LR5 veer right towards wide gap in hedge 40 yards from righthand corner of field. Through gap, go up slope in very big field on similar heading. When a group of houses (including Pie's Nest) comes into view ahead, turn left towards garden which projects into field. Follow its fence to stile hidden by thick hedge. Over this go down lefthand hedge (path LR 7) to stile to footbridge over stream in narrow band of woodland, then to second stile on other side. Follow righthand boundary to gate in corner, then cross a few yards of corner of next field to further stile (still on LR 7). Go through orchard/woodland, then across footbridge. Keep on same heading with boundaries on left through two more fields, across a metalled drive (to Hall House Farm), then a further field and a bridge (over Masefield's brook of 'liveliest delight'). Follow the lefthand boundaries in a field, woodland, then over a stile (when the spire of Ledbury Church suddenly appears in the distance). After a field, a stile,

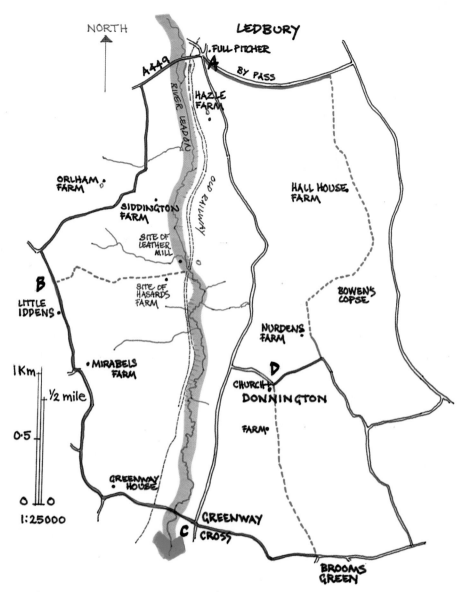

NORTH

LEDBURY

√. FULL PITCHER

A449

BY PASS

HAZLE FARM

RIVER LEADON

OLD RAILWAY

ORLHAM FARM

HALL HOUSE FARM

SIDDINGTON FARM

SITE OF LEATHER MILL

B

SITE OF HASARDS FARM

BOWEN'S COPSE

LITTLE IDDENS

NURDENS FARM

1 Km

MIRABELS FARM

D

½ mile

CHURCH

DONNINGTON

FARM

0.5

GREENWAY HOUSE

0 O

GREENWAY

1:25000

C

CROSS

BROOMS GREEN

another field, and then a stile by a gate, reach Ledbury by-pass (called Leadon Way). Follow wide verge to the left to reach the roundabout by the Full Pitcher, and the starting point.

Map: Pathfinder 1018, *Ledbury and Much Marcle*. Refreshments: Full Pitcher Hotel, Ledbury (01531 632688); Horseshoe Inn, Brooms Green (01531 890353).

# Walk 6: LEADINGTON TO THE LEADON

Many of the footpaths which criss-crossed the low-lying meadows of the Leadon Valley in the 1920s and '30s were left off the definitive map drawn up in 1948-9, and hence are no longer available. One right of way which has survived runs from Leadington to the Leadon, but no farther. Moves were afoot (1997) to bridge the river and re-instate path on east side as part of new John Masefield

multiple layers of history. The Dymock Poets, wrote the late Eric Gethyn-Jones, a local historian, 'sought the first primrose on Hasards Bank', which is on this path. The farm from which the name derived has now gone. The buildings were ruinous by the 1950s. A young couple with a plan for restoration bought them but were thwarted by a refusal of planning consent, and had to

*Pool by R. Leadon, formerly used to top up canal*

Way. The existing path to the river is worth exploring because it provides exhilarating views of Ledbury with the needle-spire of its church and of the wooded sweep of the Leadon Valley. In addition it cuts through

demolish them. Nearby was Hasards Quarry which supplied stone for the new church at Kempley, the Elizabeth Barrett Browning Institute at Ledbury, and Dymock Church.

*Little Iddens*

tioned in Domesday – survived because it impounded the whole flow of the river to turn two wheels which drove four pairs of stones. Grinding continued almost until the Second World War but by the early 1950s the massive Georgian block, four storeys high, stood derelict, and was later demolished.

The path reaches the River Leadon close to a point where the Herefordshire-Gloucestershire boundary arrives from the west and then runs south in mid-stream. Traces can be seen of the former canal (open from 1798 until 1881) which crossed the river from west to east here, as did, on a slightly different alignment, the former railway (open from 1885 until 1964) whose bridge abutments can still be seen. The pond used to top up the canal is also in existence. Just to the Herefordshire side of the county boundary stood the Leather Mill. Leather Mill Cottage (now gone) was occupied until 1946 but the mill itself ceased work as the level of the river fell when water was pumped out for the canal. Less than half a mile upstream, Hazle Mill – perhaps Ledbury's *molin. de ii solidi* (mill at two shillings) men-

*Oldfields*

## Walk 6: LEADINGTON TO THE LEADON Itinerary

1 1/2 miles (3/4 hour), starting at point B on Walk 5 (map ref. 691350), with parking on roadside. (Since space is limited, it might be preferable for this walk to be treated simply as a detour during Walk 5, on which sketch map it is shown).

From point B. on Walk 5, follow track with hedge on right, passing orchard on right, with views of Ledbury appearing to left. When track swings left by small brick barn, with newly refurbished house (Grovehill) beyond, go through gate on right. Continue in field with tall poplar hedge on left. At gap on left go through hedge and continue on original heading, now with hedge on right. Follow track down slope (Hasards Bank). At bottom, go left for a few yards, then right, through gateway. From this point the path goes straight across two fields to the river. Since an intervening fence lacks a stile, use tracks in field to

reach gate in far lefthand corner. In next field follow hedge/ditch on left (county boundary) to river, then turn right along bank for 100 yards (to reach point where path should have arrived). Behind a stout and solitary gatepost the parapet of the former railway bridge can be seen; a few yards downstream is the feeder pond for the old canal. From this point, retrace steps to Leadington.

Map: Pathfinder 108, *Ledbury and Much Marcle.*

*Dymock Church*

*Wilfrid Gibson and his wife, Geraldine, at door of Old Nailshop, Greenway*

*Lascelles Abercrombie*

*John Haines, c.1915*

*Edward Thomas, with daughter, Myfanwy, and neighbour's son.*

*Robert Frost., c.1915*

# Walk 7: DYMOCK TO BROOMS GREEN

Dymock is perhaps best known for daffodils and poets. In facts the Dymock Poets lived outside the village, though in the parish, at Leadington (Frost and Thomas), Greenway (Gibson) and Ryton (Abercrombie, Frost again, and visitors such as Rupert

*Pounds Farm*

mented from Little Iddens (see Walk 5): 'When we first came the meadows were covered with yellow daffodils and the cuckoo had just begun to sing'. The dainty wild daffodil, which rejoices in the Latin name of *Narcissus pseudonarcissus*, if much less profuse than before, still produces a spectacular 'golden gush' (the phrase is from John Haines) in springtime. However, only a few cider orchards remain, and in the whole parish there is only one cidermaker.

Dymock has a long history; indeed it must be one of the oldest settlements on the River

Brooke, W. H. Davies and John Drinkwater). Nevertheless, they have become inextricably associated with Dymock, and many of them wrote in prose or verse of the village and of the Leadon Valley. Abercrombie, in a poem written at Crowfield Farm (see Walk 8), mentions the 'golden tides of daffodils'. His wife, Catherine, wrote many years later of their stay at Ryton: 'There the earth is a rich red loam, small hills covered in fir and birch, and acres of orchards, for we were in the midst of cider-making country. The sight of the blossoming of the apple and cherry trees in spring was unforgettable, with miles and miles of daffodils pouring over the ground'. Frost com-

Leadon. It pre-dates the Romans whose town, centred where the church now stands, covered between thirty and forty acres. During the last 100 years or so, in well over a score of separate sites, a very large quantity of Roman material has come to light, and much more may well await discovery. Finds include roads, buildings, enclosures; pottery, glass, coins, and iron slag. A hook found in 1959 at the old Ann Cam School closely resembles the implement locally called a lug, which was attached to the end of a pole used to shake down apples and pears for cider and perry making. As recently as 1995 further discoveries were made when the sewage works was being extended, including the skeletal remains of three infants and five adults. The likely Roman name for Dymock has been variously rendered as *Magatonion*, *Magalonion*, *Magalonium* and *Macatonium*. Whatever the spelling, the word has been taken to mean 'place on the noble stream'. From this one might deduce that the Romans knew the Leadon as *Magalona*. A local historian, the late Eric Gethyn-Jones, has suggested that the name of Dymock might once have been *Din Mac*, meaning 'the fort of Mac(atonium)', but Ekwall in *The Concise Oxford Dictionary of English Place-names* suggests that *Dimoch*, as recorded in the Domesday Book, comes from *Ty Moch*, meaning pigsty. Pigsty or no, Dymock was a royal manor, and a place of some importance. By the thirteenth century it flourished as a market town. In the next century a long decline had begun, though most of the present church was built then. It retains some Saxon masonry and a Norman south doorway from earlier structures.

For some 400 years, ending in 1537, monks from Flaxley Abbey lived, worked and prayed at the Old Grange, which is now a golf and fitness club. Monks' Bridge, which spans the combined Preston and Kempley Brooks shortly before they join the Leadon, has retained its name ever since the monks left. Two fields away, at Pound Farm (could this once have been Pond Farm?) there is a big pool which provided the monks with fish. Mrs Phyllis Davies, who lived at The Pounds, as it is called locally, remem-

bered that tench and eels were caught there. She recalled in the 1940s seeing corncrakes in the meadows and otters (and also freshwater mussels) in the River Leadon, close to Farm Mill. This was the farm mill - hence its name - for Wilton Place (formerly called The Farm), until shortly before 1914. The last person to own both establishments was John Henry Cam Thackwell, who sold up and left the parish in 1947. The mill and its associated water channels were still there then, though later the whole building became a private house. Although the Leadon in spate can be awe-inspiring, it is not considered a greedy river like the Wye or the Severn which have the reputation of requiring a yearly victim. However, the church registers at Dymock reveal a few casualties. William Hope died in September 1787, 'killed by a fall into the river when drunk'. Two young men were swept away and drowned in November 1824 when they attempted to drive a wagon load of cider through the swollen Preston Brook at Windcross. The epitaph, to Joseph and Robert Hooper, aged respectively 28 and 18, runs:

> In perfect health we went from home,
> Not thinking that our Glass was run;
> The running floods of waters strong,
> It did our bodies over come;
> For God above who thought it fit,
> To lay our bodies in the deep:
> Now Parents dear forbear to mourn;
> We wait the resurrection morn.

# Walk 7: DYMOCK TO BROOMS GREEN Itinerary

4 miles (2 hours), starting at Dymock Church (map. ref. 700312), with parking nearby (or, in case of difficulty, in a substantial lay-by at west end of village).

A. Leave churchyard by metal kissing gate on north side. Cross field to footbridge over ditch just a few yards away from the River Leadon, which is on the right. Cross bridge in direction signed Poets' Path II, and go through short field to stile and another footbridge. In next field, keeping river on right, go to right of hedge which comes in from left, then after 50 yards go over stile on left. Turn right, and go over stile in facing hedge. Still keep river on right but when it swings sharply further to the right, continue straight across field to stile in hedge, 20 yards to right of gate. Keep to same heading in next field, along top of bank, gradually converging on lefthand boundary (and course of former railway), to reach stile by gate. Cross empty track to further stile by gate. In field, go half right to stile in hedge by double electricity pole, with barn seen beyond. Over stile, cross field to stile by bridge (Monks' Bridge). In

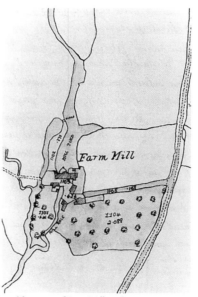

*Detail from map of Farm Mill, 1947*

huge field beyond bridge make for far righthand corner, passing to right of solitary tree in middle, and aiming to left of white house and garage. (On the left the wooded embankment of former canal is seen, with Marcle Ridge in the distance beyond it). Cross stile by gate to metalled lane and turn right (leaving at this point Poets' Path II).

B. Follow track over bridge (which spanned former railway). Immediately after cattle grid,

turn left and follow track which leaves the buildings of Pound Farm on the right. Where track is barred by gate, take stile on right and cross field to stile by gate visible among trees on far side. Go over field bridge, a few yards of meadow, and then footbridge over River Leadon. Turn right, then left through short paddock (with Farm Mill on left) to handgate. Go up drive beyond to reach road (B 4216).

C. Go left on road for 30 yards, then cross footbridge on right. In very large field (recently created by the amalgamation of several smaller ones) go half left, aiming for electricity pole. Then continue on same heading to stile and steps in bank on far side. In the field above the bank still follow same direction, gradually closing on lefthand hedge, to reach a stile to lane.

D. Turn right (having rejoined route of Poets' Path II) and follow lane for about 1/2 mile to footpath sign on right, 100 yards after Brooms Green Memorial Hall. (The Horseshoe Inn is a few yards further on). Turn right, and follow path between hedges/fences to footbridge. Cross into field, and follow righthand boundary to stile. Go through small copse, over further stile, and again follow righthand field boundary past a pond to rough stile in hedge.

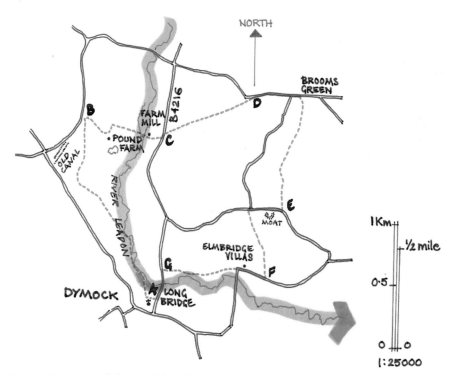

Beyond this, again follow righthand hedge to footbridge at bottom of field. Over bridge, go half left across field to reach stile to right of railings. (May Hill should have appeared ahead, on the horizon).

E. Over stile, turn right on road. (A mysterious, tree-clad moated site is beyond the lefthand hedge). After 300 yards, immediately beyond signpost on road, take stile to field by gate on left. Follow lefthand boundary to footbridge by big oak which is just inside field. Over bridge, cross big field half-right to gate to lane.

F. Turn right. After Elmbridge Villas on right, as lane swings sharply left, go ahead up steps in bank, through hedge, and over stile. In field go roughly parallel with river on left but when it winds further left keep original direction to stile in hedge. In next field, keep same heading to further stile. Then go slightly to the right, aiming to the right of a short brick culvert to reach rough stile indicated by tall footpath signs just to left of metal gate. Cross stile to road (B 4216 again).

G. Turn left. Cross Longbridge (which is really a series of bridges) and the River Leadon. Some 40 yards beyond, take stile by gate on right. Cross field half-left to reach kissing gate into churchyard and starting point.

Map: Pathfinder 1041, *Ledbury and Much Marcle*. Refreshments: Beauchamp Arms, Dymock (01531 890266); Horseshoe Inn, Brooms Green (01531 890353).

# Walk 8: DYMOCK TO KETFORD BRIDGE

Having flowed south from Ledbury, at Dymock the Leadon swings roughly eastwards to reach Ketford Bridge, some two miles away. Despite its small size Ketford (as *Chitiford*) appears in the Domesday Book.

Ketford: local doctor negotiating ford in horse and trap, c.1910, when bridge was for pedestrians only

The name means 'kite ford'. Except for a footbridge there was indeed a ford until the 1930s. A local tradition which holds that the ford is Roman was given credence about twenty years ago when in the river there a child found a phial later identified as a Roman perfume bottle. Definite sections of Roman road have been found in Dymock beneath the cricket ground and also further east past Crowfield Farm and towards Ketford. Conceivably, having crossed the Leadon at Ketford the Romans carried on to

Ashleworth and a ferry over the Severn.

George Ellis (born 1914) lived for many years at Ketford Mill (which in fact ceased working in the 1880s). As a child he walked daily to school along the Roman route. He was probably more concerned with watching kingfishers, and later with fishing for trout, dace and eels. (Advertisements for property along the river in 1919 all mention the fishing). Mr Ellis points out that the water was much higher in the Leadon than at present until two significant events: the lowering of a weir at Payford Bridge so as to drain boggy areas upstream of it, and the loss in 1947 of the mill dam across the river at Durbridge (see Walk 9). He remembers otters in the Leadon until the 1940s. These

The Beauchamp Arms, Dymock

members otters in the Leadon until the 1940s. These were hunted by members of the Wye

*Line of Roman road, east of Crowfield Farm*

Valley Otter Hunt. Mrs Phyllis Davies (see Walk 7) adds that the men carried staves and wore bright blue coats, kneebreeches and red socks. Mrs Davies's children paddled and swam in the Leadon and picnicked on its banks at the back of Cinderdine (a curious name, recorded in c. 1240 as *Ciderdine*, and meaning 'south enclosure').

Crowfield Farm, across the river from Cinderdine, was where Lascelles Abercrombie stayed for a time in 1919 on a return visit to the area before taking up an appointment as lecturer in English Literature at Liverpool University. Looking across to his beloved Ryton Firs, he saw they had been sacrificed to the war effort and wrote in a poem for his sons:

Dear boys, they've killed our woods. the ground
Now looks ashamed, to be shorn so bare;
Naked lank ridge and brooding mound
Seem shivering cowed in the April air.

The trees are back again now, handsome enough, though not as varied an those which Abercrombie conjured from his memories of the days before the First World War:

Now I breathe you again, my woods of Ryton:
Not only golden with your daffodil light
Lying in pools on the loose dusky ground
Beneath the larches, tumbling in broad rivers
Down sloping grass under the cherry trees
And birches: but among your branches clinging
A mist of that Ferrara-gold I first
Loved in those easy hours you made so green.

*An early Dymockian (see page 36)*

# Walk 8: DYMOCK TO KETFORD BRIDGE

## 4 1/2 miles (2 1/4 hours), starting and parking as in Walk 7.

A. From Wintour's Green in front of church at Dymock, follow pavement along B 4215 road towards Newent for several hundred yards. Immediately beyond stream (Still House Brook) go through kissing gate on left, by footpath sign. Cross field to stile in hedge to left of barn, ignoring stile on right to cricket pitch which is the return route. Over stile, go right to further stile-footbridge-stile, close to gate. Stay on similar line through next field, aiming for tall tree, to reach stile in hedge some 100 yards from lefthand corner.

B. Turn left on lane. Cross River Leadon by Elmbridge and follow lane as it swings right. After 1/4 mile (just after the Gloucestershire Wildlife Trust's daffodil meadow) turn right at drive to Field House. Take stile in fence on left of drive and follow lefthand hedge. After 100 yards cross footbridge and stile on left into field. *At this point it is possible to go straight on instead, re-cross the river by a footbridge, and so greatly abbreviate the walk.* Cross field obliquely to right, to stile by river. Go through old orchard, with Cinderdine Cottage on left and river on right, then over double stile. Continue on same heading to further stile by river bank then another in fence. Beyond that, make for righthand corner of field to stile and footbridge, then pass with river under motorway (M 50). Beyond cross field half-left, aiming to right of group of willow trees. Cross footbridge over brook and go up slope in field. At boundary fence (to Callow Farm) turn left. *A right turn at this point would provide a further possibility for a short-cut.* Go with fence on right through gate and over stile by double gate to reach a track. Turn right, passing barns on right, and following track as it swings left uphill to very large field. Cross this, making to left of greenhouses seen beyond. (The wood behind

these is Ryton Firs). Go through gap in hedge by footpath sign to reach lane.

C. Turn right. Follow lane, which rapidly becomes deeply sunken, past Ketford Mill (now simply a dwelling), and turn right to re-cross River Leadon by Ketford Bridge. Turn right on far side along track marked by bridleway sign. After about 100 yards go through gate on right into field, and follow lefthand boundary round houses through gap in fence/hedge and on to hunting gate by holly tree. Follow rough track along side of bank, with precipitate drop on right (and desultory watercourse beyond). Go through metal gate with symbol of Gloucestershire Farming Wildlife Advisory Group (FWAG), and then through hunting gate into open field. Keep same line across field (with views of Marcle Ridge appearing ahead, and of the Malvern Hills to the right). *At hunting gate path from Callow Farm comes in from right.* Go through hunting gate into field and follow lefthand hedge to further gate. Continue on track between hedges over motorway, then through three gates at Crowfield Farm to reach metalled lane (Crowfield Lane).

D. Follow lane. *After a few hundred yards path from Field House/Vell Mill comes in from right.* Continue to T-junction. Go up steps in facing bank, and over stile in hedge. In field, aim just to left of church spire. Cross stile in fence on left, then keep original line to further stile in hedge. On cricket ground, follow righthand boundary swinging a few yards left at far end to stile in fence. Beyond, make for apex of projecting hedge on left, then turn left beyond it to reach kissing gate to road (B4215). Turn right to return to starting point.

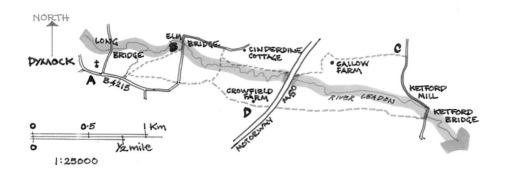

*T.B. Thompson of Goodrich, Master of Wye Valley Otter Hounds, 1925*

Map: Pathfinder 1041, *Ledbury and Much Marcle*. Refreshments: Beauchamp Arms, Dymock (01531 890266).

# Walk 9: KETFORD TO PAUNTLEY

A mile below Ketford Bridge the Leadon flows into a spectacular gorge, which broadens into a secluded valley. Buzzards mew as they wheel over the woods. Herons prowl the pools and wild geese graze the grassy banks. To the south there are lush orchards, and even vineyards. In spring, wild daffodils abound, together with bluebells, ramsons, celandines, violets, anemones and dog's mercury. After exploring this

*Durbridge Mill and Farm*

stretch of the river with Robert Frost, John Haines wrote of 'the unusual flowers .... the Ladies' Tresses, the Little Teasel, the Spreading Campanula, loveliest of harebells, and the queer things that grew in the salt springs that burst out of the Leadon'. Elsewhere, he explained that the 'queer things' were Brooklime and Sea Clubrush. One salt spring emerges from the slope above the Leadon near the footbridge (once known as Huntsman's Bridge) downstream from Durbridge, and some of Haines's flowers are still to be found there.

Stocks Mill (called Harridge Mill on a map of 1831) stood on the other side of the river from the spring, and was driven by a stream. The mill has now completely disappeared. In 1549 the d'Abitots of Redmarley owned a mill at Durbridge (the name means 'deer

bridge'), and the sandstone building (or its descendant) is still there, its iron water-wheel in place though no longer working. The mill's productive life came to a sudden and spectacular end in 1947 when the dam and sluices were swept away by disastrous floods caused by the rapid thawing of a record snowfall. The presence of a hop kiln points to the brewing of beer here, and the mill certainly drove a scratcher used to break up apples for cider-making. As at Durbridge, so at Payford the mill sustained damage in 1947: its gates were destroyed, and part of the cast-iron wheel carried away. Both these (the wheel bears the name 'Dimmock' which may indicate the maker or the place of making) were made good in the 1980s by Mr John Moakes, but the river authority forbade the replacement of the weir because of its potential effect on water levels. Mr Moakes recalls how, even so, the Leadon frequently rose through his floor. An earlier restoration was carried out by the artist, Robert Herdman-Smith (1879-1932), who lived there in the 1920s. He was succeeded as owner by an Eton schoolmaster who used the mill as a holiday home. During the Second World War it served as a school for refugee children from France and Belgium who were accommodated at Pauntley Court.

Their teacher was a Monsieur V. Pollet. The mill's earlier history awaits documentation. It goes back at least to 1777, when the building appeared on Isaac Taylor's map of Gloucestershire.

On May Eve people used to walk the six miles from Newent to Payford Bridge for an annual bout of internal spring cleaning. They gathered wood, made fires, and sat round them till dawn. Then they heated water and, 'having drunk a number of horns full of it, they used to run round a field in the shape of a figure eight until the desired result was obtained'. The curious practice came to an end early this century not because those involved tired of it but since farmers were unhappy about damage caused to their hedge and fences by the wood gatherers. Another local custom relating to 5 January, the eve of Epiphany, was described by the historian, T.D.Fosbrooke, in 1807 when it had already disappeared:

In the parish of Pauntley, and the surrounding neighbourhood, the servants of each farmer formerly assembled together in one of the fields that had been sown with wheat. At the end of twelve lands, they made twelve fires in a row with straw around one of which, much larger than the rest, they drank a

*Payford Mill, photographed in 1940s by Belgian refugee, V.Pollet*

cheerful glass of cider to their master's health, and success to the future harvest; then, returning home, they feasted on cakes soaked in cider, which they claimed as a reward for their past labours in sowing the grain.

A tradition which has obstinately survived is the success story of Dick Whittington and his cat. It seems highly likely that Dick was born at Pauntley Court (in the 1350s) and baptised at the nearby Norman church of St John, which has many other associations with the Whittington family. The Whittingtons owned Pauntley Court from 1311 until 1546. Part of the present house and the dovecot survive from their time. In the 1930s the Court (now a private house not open to the public) was 'The Gloucestershire Home for Wayfarers'. John Masefield, who had known what it was like to be down and out, supported the venture. The shell of Pauntley Mill still stands near the Court. It was driven by a stream from Collinpark Wood (see Walk 10), another of the Leadon's tributaries. This may or may not have been the mill worth 7s. 6d. mentioned in Domesday as belonging to Ansfrid de Cormeilles whose estates in the locality included land at Ketford and Durbridge as well as Pauntley.

## Walk 9: KETFORD TO PAUNTLEY

5 1/2 miles (2¾ hours), starting at Ketford Bridge (map ref. 730308 and parking in lay-by immediately to north of bridge.

A. Take track indicated by bridleway sign to north of bridge, through small metal gate by cattle grid. Follow fence on right, with River Leadon further right, and continue to do so when track bears left. Go through gates and follow righthand hedges in next two fields. Continue on same heading after gate to third field, though now with hedge on left. Follow track through gate as it winds past farm (Cut Mill), to right of buildings, then in between house and bungalow. Ignoring first a footpath to left and then a bridleway (where the return route rejoins), keep on track as it swings right. Follow fence on right, go through gate, and then uphill, passing house on left, with deep river gorge starting to appear on right. At junction at top of slope, turn right, and follow track downhill. Go through gate, pass between the buildings of Durbridge Farm and Mill, and then go through another gate. Follow track to right and cross Leadon by gated bridge. On far side, turn left, and follow river on left. (Wooded cliff on right is covered with wild daffodils in spring). At end of wood go through small gate into field. Cross to big gate on far side, veering slightly to left and passing to left of large pond associated with

former Stocks Mill, with footbridge over river further to left, formerly known as Huntsman's Bridge. The salt spring is beyond the footbridge, to the left). In field beyond pond, follow lefthand hedge, above the river, and at far end, a few yards up the slope from the lefthand corner, go through hunting gate. Continue on previous heading through rough field, then along steep wooded bank. As scrub and trees thin, and modern houses appear in view, turn right through hawthorn trees, take gate into field, and head for far lefthand corner, to the right of house (Keeper's Cottage) and towards lefthand end of row of poplars. Go through gate on to track, and short distance up track to road.

B. Turn right up hill. After 200 yards, turn left (signed Pauntley Church). Follow lane downhill to an open space with Pauntley Church on right and Pauntley Court on left. Immediately before the two pillars marking the drive to the Court, turn left down grassy track, through double gate. Follow track as it swings left, away from the Court. With river on right follow track to rough stile by gate. In fields follow fence on left. At far end go through gate to road.

C. Turn right. Cross Payford Bridge, with its metal railings, and immediately turn left into lane. (Payford Mill soon comes into view on left). Go up lane, past the imposing Murrell's End Farm. At road junction go straight ahead through gate by bridleway sign into field. Follow lefthand hedge. Go through gap (waymarked) in sandstone, and through hunting gate into field. Follow lefthand fence to another hunting gate. Turn right on track to Cut Mill Farm, and follow first part of outward route back to starting point at Ketford Bridge.

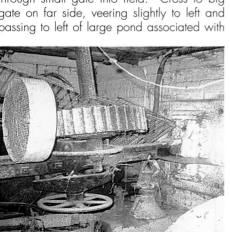
*Machinery at Payford Mill, 1970s*

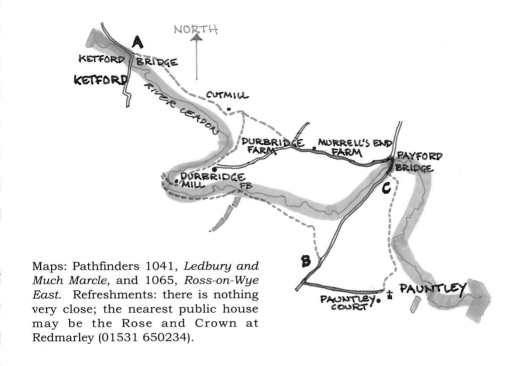

Maps: Pathfinders 1041, *Ledbury and Much Marcle*, and 1065, *Ross-on-Wye East*. Refreshments: there is nothing very close; the nearest public house may be the Rose and Crown at Redmarley (01531 650234).

*Remains of weir at Durbridge, 1970s*

# Walk 10: ROUND UPLEADON

Upleadon means simply a place farther up the Leadon; that is, beyond Highleadon, which in turn signifies the Leadon of the *hiwan* (members of a religious house, in this case a group of monks from Gloucester Abbey). The manor of *Ledene*, including both Upleadon and Highleadon, was granted by William the Conqueror to Walter de Lacy, who then presented it to St Peter's Abbey at Gloucester. We know from Domesday Book that the manor included a mill worth four shillings. This, the forerunner of the present building, drew on the combined waters of the Leadon and its tributary, the Glynch Brook, which rises near Eastnor in Herefordshire. Grinding by water power ended early this century, but the Dunn brothers of Upleadon Court, using electricity, continued to employ the mill to grind corn for cattle feed until 1995. The external undershot

*Mill and pool at Upleadon*

wheel with its iron buckets is still in place. Water power probably played a part in Upleadon's iron industry, which was first recorded some three hundred years ago.

*R.Leadon near Upleadon*

Names of local fields include Burnt Ground, Burnt Hill, Cinder Fields and Pit Field. Forge Lane runs past the mill, which on the first Ordnance Survey map of 1831 is marked as Forge Mill.

Much of the modern village has preferred the higher ground of Eden's Hill, leaving close to the river the ancient nucleus of church, mill and court. To escape perennial floods the church

*Bridge over R.Leadon near Everes's Farm*

stands on a great clay mound raised probably in Saxon times. Despite many restorations the building remains simple and attractive. Some Norman work survives – especially the north doorway – but the church's chief glory must be the fine timber-framed tower of about 1500. A curious feature, perhaps intended to ward off evil influence, is the stone carving of a pig's head set in the east side of the chancel arch. Eden's Hill, crowned by sessile oaks, is partly owned by the National Trust. Collinpark Wood, the property of Gloucestershire Wildlife Trust, is a Site of Special Scientific Interest, largely because of its wealth of small-leaved limes whose presence indicates ancient woodland. There are signs of coppicing, the ancient technique of rotational cutting back which ensured a never-ending supply of timber.

*Upleadon Church*

# Walk 10: UPLEADON

6 miles (3 hours), starting near Upleadon Church (map ref. 769270), with parking on roadside verges.

A. Go through gate by pond on side of road opposite drive to Upleadon Church and Court. Cross field to gate in hedge by big oak tree. Keep on same line through next field to gate, then across narrow meadow to reach footbridge over River Leadon. On other side cross to apex of field where two sets of gates and bridges lead over watercourses. Go ahead through wooden gates and cross stone bridge over Glynch Brook. Go up slope towards far side of next field, and cross hedge and ditch by footbridge. Cross next field with brook on left to reach stile in hedge to left of clump of trees. Then go to far left corner of a short, uneven field to reach gate to road.

B. Turn left. Go along lane, initially with brook still on left, past drive to Stanbrook Stud Farm on left, and up rise. By footpath sign turn left down drive of house (Shalimar), and start following the waymarks of the Whitmore Way (a series of walks round Corse and Staunton established in 1992 in memory of a local rambler, John Whitmore), with fence/hedge on right. Beyond the house go to right of big wooden shed, with hedge on right. Past shed, follow track between two hedges. Shortly after sharp bend to right, turn right at junction of tracks. At next junction, turn left along metalled road, going away from Little Brierley Farm. Follow road to T-junction. Turn left, leaving house (Birchfield) on right. (Shortly after this, the Whitmore Way goes off to right). Continue on lane, which soon becomes a track, passing Sladbrook Farm on the left (with May Hill visible beyond) and the red-brick ruin of Downing Farm on the right.

C. Where the way is barred by a metal gate, take stile on right. Go for 100 yards between hedges to further stile. Beyond, follow hedge on right to another stile. Over this, aim for hedge on far side seen through gap in tall trees. Cross footbridge over stream. In field, go diagonally left up slope to gap in hedge (with gable end of house seen beyond: this is Everes's Farm, recorded in 1830 as Evoras Farm). Cross next field on same line to further gate. Turn left of big pool in front of house and pass along track between barns and through gate. Continue on track and cross the Leadon by old stone bridge, then bear left to footbridge over stream. On other side turn right along sunken path with hedge and stream bed on right. Where the long field comes to a narrow end, go through the hedge (not easy, though there is a sort of gap), cross a dry ditch, and continue in next field on former heading with hedge, stream bed and shortly a wood (Collinpark Wood) on right.

D. Where a spur of the wood projects to the left the map shows that the path continues straight through it on the same heading. However, there is no trace of a path on this line in the wood, and it seems that walkers go round the corner of the wood and through a gate on the right into a field, where they proceed with the wood's boundary on their right. Where this swings sharply right, go ahead and follow lefthand hedge to far corner of field. There, cross stile by gate and follow track (initially sunken) to left, along shoulder of Eden's Hill.

E. At road, turn left. After 50 yards take stile on right into field. Follow righthand hedge but when this veers right go ahead across field, slightly to left, to pass through wide gateway in hedge opposite. Go half left across next field to stile in hedge by oak tree. In next field, gradually diverge from hedge on left to reach gap in facing hedge beyond solitary old

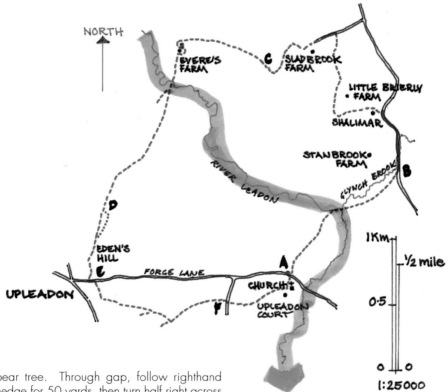

pear tree. Through gap, follow righthand hedge for 50 yards, then turn half right across field, aiming to left of white house. Cross bridge and cattle grid and turn sharp left. Keeping hedge and watercourse on left and barns and stables on right, go 100 yards to stile. In field beyond, follow lefthand hedge to far lefthand corner. Take footbridge on left into old orchard. Go across orchard to gate in hedge on far side. Then cross two fields (with tower of Upleadon Church seen in distance) on more or less same line to reach gate leading to road.

F. Cross road to stile on other side. Follow lefthand hedge through two fields, then follow track through farm buildings at Upleadon Court to reach church, and starting point.

Map: Pathfinder 10659, *Ross-on-Wye East*. Refreshments: none close; nearest, probably one of the three public houses in Hartpury - Canning Arms (01452 700275), Royal Exchange (01452 700273) or Watersmeet (01452 700138) - or the Swan Inn, Staunton (01452 840323).

# Walk 11: UPLEADON TO MALSWICK MILL

Immediately to the south of Upleadon, access to the river is not easy. In the two miles to Hartpury Mill (see Walk 12) no road approaches the Leadon. One footpath, from Red Hill to Limbury, should do so, but at present it lacks a bridge. However, Walk 11 is very much in the Leadon Valley, with fine views of May Hill. It includes an excursion to one of the Leadon's main tributaries, the Ell Brook (ell here is a corruption of elm), which in turn is formed from several streams rising in Kilcot and Gorsley Woods. The Ell has its own pleasant valley, recently saved from obliteration when strong local opposition combined with central shortage of money to persuade the government to drop a misguided plan to drive a dual carriageway

through it. The brook powered several mills. Crookes Mill at Oxenhall was demolished in 1896 to make way for a pumping station. Cleeve Mill, just outside Newent, stands on foundations which could date from Norman times. It worked until at least 1959, water power being supplemented by an oil engine and later an electric motor, to grind animal food. A little downstream Okle Pitcher Mill became a private house in the 1930s. The nearby Brass Mill is now also a dwelling, much of its machinery having been sold for scrap during the Second World War. The last miller, named Fawkes, claimed to be a descendant of Guy Fawkes, and the place was known locally as Fawkes's Mill. The earlier name must derive from brass wire draw-

*Malswick Mill*

*May Hill, seen from near Hartpury Church*

ing carried on there for the pin-making factories of Gloucester.

The last mill on the Ell Brook, which, oddly, from this point to its confluence with the Leadon changes its name to Leachford Brook, is Malswick Mill. 'In 1945', wrote Gwladys Davies, 'this mill was still working and one could often hear its wheel rumbling and splashing under the low archway right against the main road. During the war Mrs Perry, the wife of the miller continued the milling and even on some rush occasions stayed up all night to make sure the provender was ground'. By 1965 the mill had ceased working. The buildings, recently extended, are now a private house though parts of the sluices and mill race can still be seen. This walk again crosses and re-crosses the line of the former canal and railway. It also passes many venerable farms, some now purely residential, others very much in production. Middletown was first recorded in 1347, Hay Farm (from the Old English, *haeg*, enclosure) even earlier, in 1086. Moat Farm received a mention in 1779, but may well be older.

In summer the hedgerows are full of flowers, including wild hops, hypericum and honeysuckle. Jack-go-to-bed can also be seen, its name reflecting a belief that the flower opens early in the morning and closes at midday.

# Walk 11: UPLEADON TO MALSWICK MILL

4 miles (2 hours), starting as in Walk 10. This walk goes through four farmyards and three gardens,

A. From Upleadon Church follow track westward past barns, with fence on right. After last barn go through wide metal gate into field and follow righthand hedge to further gate. Keep same heading to far righthand corner of next field. Turn left here, ignoring stile to road. Follow righthand hedge to corner of field and cross footbridge, narrow strip of woodland, and second footbridge. In next field, follow fence with new hedge on right, past back of Middletown Farm, to stile. Cross paddock obliquely to right to reach further stile and footbridge. Go straight through orchard/garden of Bayton's Farm, keeping roughly parallel with lefthand boundary to reach fence on far side. Turn right within this fence, ignoring stile over which leads to another path, and follow it to a track. Join the track and follow it to a road.

B. Turn right. After 200 yards go through gate on left by footpath sign. Follow righthand boundary in field to rough stile in hedge by watercourse in bottom righthand corner. Bear left in next field to reach hedge, then follow this to farm (The Reddings, which means clearings). Go through farm yard by series of gates to reach road.

C. Turn left. After 100 yards, immediately past house (Raysheil), turn right on to signed track. Follow this for 1/4 mile, then pass to the right of the half-timbered Hay Farm and its buildings. At the end of a row of poplars on the right, go through gate into field. Continue on previous heading, now with fence on left. Go over bridge and through gate. Cross short paddock then go through gate and over bridge spanning Ell Brook. Keep same line over short lawn, then cross leat of Malswick Mill by metal footbridge. Follow narrow path between hedges to road. (This is the busy B4215, so care is needed).

D. Go left for a few yards, then cross road in front of mill house to stile (which may be half-hidden) in hedge. In field, follow lefthand hedge. Beyond top of slope, just before a deep pit, go through gate on left. Turn right in field and follow hedge on right. Go up embankment of former railway to stile. Cross small paddock to further stile. Turn left on track which runs on broad strip of land between two hedges. Follow track down slope, and as the barns of Moat Farm come into view ahead, go through gate in hedge on right. Turn left in field, and follow hedge on left with orchard beyond. At bottom of field go through gate and turn left, with orchard hedge still on left. In corner of field go through gate ahead (not the one on left), and pass to the right of Moat Farmhouse. Keep on same heading past various buildings. When the metalled farm road swings sharply left, go ahead over rickety metal gate in hedge (with strand of barbed wire beyond) into field. Bear right towards wide gap in hedge on right, but do not go through gap; turn left with hedge on right (crossing route of railway once more) and go to gate to road (B 4215 again).

E. Go right for few yards on road, then turn left through gate into field. Cross towards small wood, with waymark on post. At post, turn right and follow boundary of wood. At top of field go through gap on left into wood, and turn right to follow track inside with fence on right. When a garden fence appears on left, follow this, even though it may seem to be leading to a dead end. The footpath goes immediately to the right of a house, through the front garden (with stones marking the way along the side of lawn), and emerges via a small gate on to lane.

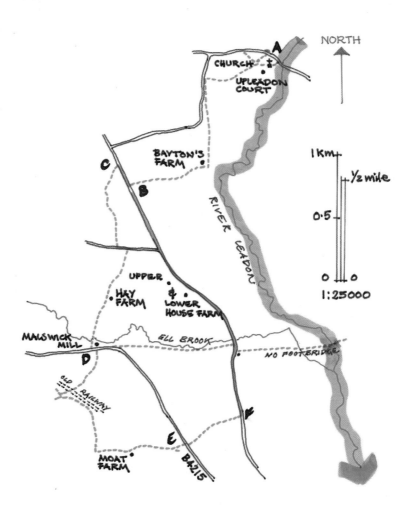

NORTH

1 Km
½ mile
0·5
0
1:25000

F. Turn left on road, with view of the Malverns shortly appearing ahead. After about 1/4 mile re-cross the Ell Brook (or Leachford Brook, as it now is). Continue for 55 mile more along lane, passing in succession Lower and Upper House Farms and the turning to Okle Green (Okle means oak clearing), all on the left. (The River Leadon is only a field or two away to the right, though unfortunately not visible from the road). By a house on the right (The Homestead), reach point B, and turn to right to return to starting point by first part of outward route. *Alternatively, continue on road, turning right and then right again, to reach starting point.*

Map: Pathfinder 1065, *Ross-on-Wye East.* Refreshments: as Walk 11.

# Walk 12: HARTPURY TO RUDFORD

Hartpury was once known as 'five ends and no middle', the reference being to the constituent hamlets of Corse End, Butters End, Moor End, Blackwells End and Murrells End. The name, meaning 'tree of hard pears', was first recorded in c. 1155, as *Hardepirer*. At Hartpury, as at Upleadon, the modern village has forsaken its ancient centre of mill, court and church. There is an imposing tithe-barn, dating from the fourteenth century. The soaring tower of the spacious church of St Mary is of the same period, though the building itself is of Norman origin. The timber-work of the outer doorway is, according to H. J. Massingham, 'one of the most beautiful pieces of local craftsmanship to be seen even along the banks of the Severn.' St Mary's belonged to the monks of St Peter's Abbey (which is now the cathedral) at Gloucester, and Abbot's Place is the former name of the adjacent Hartpury Court. The monks alone owned the mill at Hartpury (sometimes confusingly termed Highleadon Mill) until 1267, when it passed into manorial hands. The present three-storey building of red-brick stands on massive stone foundations which may go back to those early times.

With two wheels driven by the Leadon, one on either side, the mill worked until 1939, when, on the grounds that it contributed to flooding, the Severn Catchment Board decreed that the dam should be lowered by two feet and the wheels scrapped. On the pleading of the last miller, Gilbert Vallender, one wheel was left *in situ*, its lower buckets removed and its rim fixed in concrete. No machinery remains inside, though it is reported that the present owners are bent on full restoration.

*Hartpury Mill, 1970s*

Downstream from Hartpury Mill is Barber's Bridge but the settlement, once boasting a railway station, stands well above the Leadon. Its name, first recorded in 1830, may come from a bridge over the Red Brook or over the former canal.

In the 1790s as they were cutting the canal navvies unearthed skeletons at this place on the west bank of the Leadon. Then in 1868 workmen removing a hillock so as to fill in a pool found 86 more skeletons which were reburied at a spot later marked by the erection of an obelisk. W.P.Price, MP, of Tibberton Court, realised that these were the remains of royalist Welshmen slain by parliamentary troops in 1643. He had heard this

*Barber's Bridge Station, c.1920*

from Hannah Taylor, daughter of a blacksmith born in 1772, whose father had passed on stories from his grandfather, who had witnessed the Civil War battle. Many times when she had walked across the fields to Hartpury, said Hannah, her father told her that if certain mounds were disturbed the bones of the vanquished Welshmen would come to light. The Red Brook owed its name to the slaughter; and in spring, people said, a Cranesbill flower bloomed in the meadows for every Welshman slain. Even Barber's Bridge was called Barbarous Bridge. Parliamentary casualties, it seems, were buried in consecrated ground: the churchyard at Rudford or even (probably in the case of

officers) beneath the chancel of the church itself, where a commemoratory service for all the victims was held 350 years on, in 1993. The early Norman building is unfortunately inaccessible to visitors, since it is kept locked. The adjacent mill, recorded in the Domesday Book, continued working for eight centuries. For many years now it has been a private house. The river must once have been fordable here – Rudford means 'reedy ford' – but a fine footbridge on high piers erected in the mid-1990s, allows the walker to cross dry-shod. This is the last public bridge before the Leadon joins the Severn.

# Walk 12: HARTPURY TO RUDFORD

## 5 1/2 miles (2 3/4 hours), starting at Hartpury Church (map ref. 780237), where there is ample parking.

A. Go south on lane between church and tithe barn for just under 1/2 mile. Shortly after crossing a watercourse, turn right through metal kissing gate. Cross big field, heading to left of belt of trees. At far side go through gate on left and continue on original heading for 10 yards, crossing a track to stile in fence. Bear left across next field to stile in far lefthand corner, to left of wire fence. Over stile, follow righthand hedge down slope and under power lines. Go through hedge in bottom righthand corner and over stile. Cross next field half left to footbridge over River Leadon. On other side turn left and cross corner of field to stile, grassy bridge over brook (Red Brook), and second stile. In field, follow ditch on left but as it swings further left go up slope, keeping buildings of Bridge Farm on right, to reach gate to road (B 4215) 50 yards to left of obelisk. (This is a permissive deviation from the definitive line).

B. Turn right on road. *A short cut at this point is possible by turning left instead of right for a few yards, and then taking stile on left which gives access to former railway by right of way created in 1994. The track can be followed to Rudford.* After turning right, after about 100 yards, opposite the front of Bridge Farm, cross to side road. Turn left along it, and cross bridge over former railway, with old Barber's Bridge station buildings on right. Over bridge, take stile on right into field. Follow righthand hedges/fence. Go through gap into field and follow lefthand boundary to gate.

*Obelisk at Barber's Bridge*

Through gate turn left on to wide concrete path at Bovone Farm, and follow this past kitchen garden and then in front of farmhouse. (The route waymarked here differs from that shown on O.S. map). Keep on track (Bovone Lane) to reach road at Tibberton.

C. Turn left. Follow road through Cuckold's Ash for about 1/4 mile, ignoring bridleway on right opposite The Forge, and take signed footpath on right by a bungalow, through gate. Go down grassy track to stile in lefthand hedge. Cross corner of field to another stile. Go half left in next field to stile in hedge. Cross brook by field bridge. Keep same line across big field, through gap in hedge, and then in further field, converging on lefthand hedge. Go down bank to kissing gate leading to road (B 4215). (Take great care here since road is very busy and dense hedge obscures vision).

D. Cross to lane opposite, signed Rudford Church. Follow sunken lane, overhung by trees, cross bridge over former railway, immediately before which alternative route from point B.comes in from left. Between Rudford Church on left and former mill on right, take signed track. Follow this to left to cross bridge over Tibberton Brook, then right to cross River Leadon by high footbridge. In field, cross to righthand corner, passing beneath power lines, to reach footbridge over ditch. Beyond this, go up flight

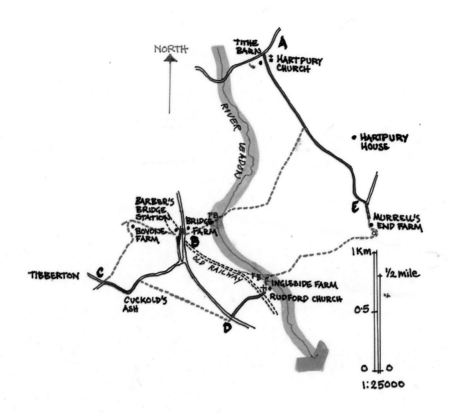

of steps in steep bank ahead, then cross field towards electricity pole, and on to far righthand corner. Over stile, follow track with hedge on left. Continue on waymarked track as it zigzags round farm buildings at Murrell's End, finally passing to left of barns to reach road.

E. Turn left. *At this point it is possible to turn right to join Walk 13 and to follow it for 5 miles to its common starting point with Walk 12.* After turning left, turn left again within a few yards, and follow road for just under a mile to reach starting point by Hartpury Church.

Map: Pathfinder 1065, *Ross-on-Wye East.* Refreshments: inns at Hartpury (see Walk 11).

*59*

# Walk 13: HARTPURY TO MAISEMORE

'Scratch Gloucestershire and find Rome', says the adage, which certainly holds true for the track on the east bank of the Leadon from Hartpury's Murrell's End to Maisemore, along the course of which traces of Roman paving have been found in several places. On some older O.S. maps the route is labelled Roman Way. The local people call it Bar Lane, which may indicate that wild pigs once roamed here, because *bar* in Old English means boar. At Maisemore two Roman ways must have met (or diverged, depending on the direction taken), Bar Lane, to Highleadon and Newent,

O, lovely City! All the valley blue
Covers thee like a garment of soft art, [heart
Harbour of peace, haven for contented and high
Desire is satisfied, sorrow finds salve in you.

As a child, Ivor Gurney frequently walked with his father from Gloucester to visit his grandparents at Spring Hill, Maisemore, where his father had been born. The people there were known for certain expressions, such as 'in Rumble's Meadow' (meaning 'in the wrong') and 'to cry Bill Tinker' ('to make a great noise'). As in many parishes, there are some interesting names for fields and other

*Picnic on the banks of the Leadon, 1940s*

the Old Gloucester Road to Ledbury. This travels on high ground, overlooking the Severn on one side and the Leadon on the other. On its way north from Maisemore the road passes Spring Hill with its wide views. Ivor Gurney (1890-1937) watched Gloucester from this vantage point before writing the poem, 'Above Maisemore', which begins:

places in Maisemore, such as Puck Pit, Farmer's Horn, Slough Wash Hill, Sinklose, Woodcroft Hides, Swingley, Wabblidge Hill, Highridden Hill and Crockley.

The Feast of St Giles, patron saint of the Church, used to be celebrated on the first Sunday in September with games of wrestling, cudgel fights, sack races and smock running. At Christmas the villagers sang their own version of the wassail song:

We've been a-wassailing all over the town;
Our bread it is white and our ale it is brown.
Our bowl it is made of the sycamore tree,
And a wassailing bowl we drink unto thee.

(Chorus)
Wassail, wassail, our jolly wassail,
And joy shall go with our jolly wassail.

Here's a health to the ox and to his old head,
Here's wishing our master a good loaf of bread;
A good loaf of bread, that may we all see,
And a wassailing bowl we drink unto thee.

Here's a health to the ox and to his right eye,
Here's wishing our master a good Christmas
pie;
A good Christmas pie, that we may all see,
And a wassailing bowl we drink unto thee.

Here's a health to the ox and to his old horn,
Here's wishing our master a good crop of corn;
A good crop of corn, that we may all see,
And a wassailing bowl we drink unto thee.

Here's a health to the ox and to his old tail,
Here's wishing our master a good tap of ale;
A good tap of ale, that we may all see,
And a wassailing bowl we drink unto thee,

There was an old woman who had an old cow;
To keep her cow warm she did not know how,
So she builded a barn to keep her cow warm,
And a drop of good liquor will do us no harm.

Come butler now bring us a bowl of your best,
And we'll hope that your soul in heaven may
rest,
But if you don't bring us a bowl of your small,
Down will go butler, bowl and all.

These words were recorded by Rev.A.R.Winnington-Ingram, rector of Lassington a century ago.

Miss Zoë Nelmes was born at Maisemore, where her father was village blacksmith from 1916 until 1941, and has lived there all her life. She recollects how farmers brought horses along the Roman road from Hartpury to have them shod in her father's smithy. Others drove horses down Blacksmith's Lane in the other direction so that they might quench their thirst in the Leadon. The blacksmith himself, when the well ran dry in time of drought, would go down for water with a yoke and two pails. Local children learned to swim in the river. Miss Nelmes remembers: 'The August school holiday was spent here having picnics, swimming and the boys camping'. Her niece, Mrs E.J.Daykin, has similar memories of summers in the late 1950s: 'Most Sunday afternoons we had a picnic on the banks of the River Leadon. Lots of families went and everyone mixed together and had a great time. We collected our drinking water from a spring along the river bank'. Miss Nelmes also recalls: 'Between Maisemore and Hartpury was a wooden bridge, known as the Hunting Bridge, to allow the hunt access to Highnam and Lassington Woods. I believe it was given and maintained by the Gordon Canning Family of Hartpury House, now the Agricultural College. I can recollect seeing it in a very dilapidated state, and it has now disappeared altogether'.

# Walk 13: HARTPURY TO MAISEMORE Itinerary
## 6 miles (3 hours), starting as Walk 12.

A. Go south on lane between church and tithe barn for 1 mile, and at first junction turn right past no through road sign towards Murrell's End. Just before the brick gate pillars of Murrell's End House, go through gate on left and follow tree-lined sunken track (Bar Lane). Shortly after crossing bridge over stream, go through gate on right into field and continue with hedge on left. Just before big pond, turn left through gap in hedge, and immediately bear right. In righthand corner of field go through gap in hedge to next field, and at the end of that, through hunting gate. Continue on same heading, still with hedge on right, and River Leadon only a few yards beyond it. Go through big gate, and up slope to hunting gate. (Views of the Cotswold ridge ap-

B. Turn right, then, after 100 yards, left down Gloucester Old Road. *Those wishing to visit the White Hart Inn will follow A 417 downhill for mile before returning to this point to continue walk.* At crossroads on Old Road turn left towards Hartpury. (Maisemore Church is seen to right at this point). Follow road for just over half a mile. After house on right (Upper Hyde), ignore path sign on left with symbol of walking figure, but turn left through gate at next sign, marked Public Footpath. Go up field with hedge on right for about 100 yards, then through gate on right. Cross next field obliquely to right to gate in dip, then go up slope neyond on same heading to further gate on right. Through this, follow hedge on left to stile on left, just beyond flagpole. Follow hedge on left through garden where path is

*Bathing in the Leadon near Maisemore, 1940s*

pear ahead, and the river veers away to the right). Go on, still with hedge on right, through waymarked hunting gate. After about 100 yards between hedges, go through another hunting gate and turn left on track, which becomes Blacksmith's Lane, and leads to road (A 417) at Maisemore.

marked by white pegs, then go ahead to road. Turn left on road, with Rising Sun Inn (locally known as the Salt Box) on the left. Go downhill on Hiam's Lane to road (A 417). Cross to Dent's Lane, opposite. Just beyond Blenheim Cottage, turn right. Follow drive with hedge on right. Go

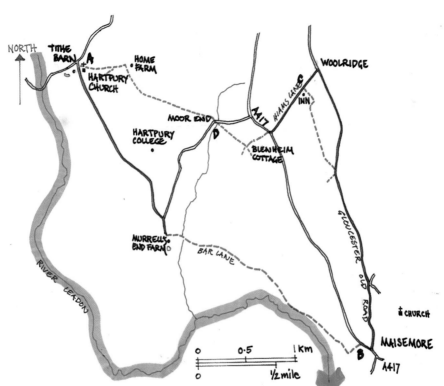

to right of one garage, then to left of another, to reach stile leading to Darley Wood. Follow fenced path to another stile. In field follow righthand fence to stile by gate, to reach road at Moor End.

C. Turn left. After 50 yards, where road turns left by cottage with rounded end, turn right. After 50 yards more, turn left, with hedge on left. When hedge bends further left, go straight over big field, making for far righthand corner to stile by gate in big gap between clump of trees on left and single specimen on right (The buildings of Hartpury College are seen away to the left). A few yards further on, go over ladder-stile by gate and follow track in field parallel with righthand boundary. After a big pond on the left, with May Hill visible beyond, go through kissing gate by large gate in righthand corner of field. Some 40 yards

further on, go over stile on left. Turn right in field and go up slope, roughly parallel with righthand fence, aiming to the left of buildings (Home Farm) and cottages on the skyline. Just beyond the buildings, go right to white metal gate which gives access to drive. Turn left. After some 250 yards go up steps on right to stile in hedge. In field, go obliquely left down slopes heading for tower of Hartpury Church. Go over stile by gate, and then to the right to enter churchyard by stile in corner. Go through churchyard to reach starting point.

Maps: Pathfinders 1065, *Ross-on-Wye East* and 1066, *Cheltenham*. Refreshments: White Hart Inn, Maisemore (01452 526349); Rising Sun Inn, Hiam's Lane, Hartpury (01452 700392).

# Walk 14: HIGHNAM, LASSINGTON AND OVER

John Haines described the last stretch of the Leadon as 'a dirty ditch'. Fortunately, this is no longer true, though one must say that the river does come to an ignominious end, its confluence with the Severn controlled by big, unsightly sluices.

The final miles lie between Maisemore (see Walk 13) on the east bank and Lassington on the west. Lassington has a small size but a considerable history, with an appearance in Domesday as *Lessedune*, which means 'lesser hill', presumably by contrast with the slightly more imposing heights across the river above Maisemore.

The church of St Oswald is now reduced to an eleventh century

*Lassington Church*

tower only, the nave, rebuilt in 1875. having been demolished exactly a hundred years later. The dead, sleeping peacefully in their Saxon mound, include James Byett, who died in 1812 at the age of 59:

My life is past my work is done
I now at last to rest am gone
In silent grave I here remain
Till Soul and Body meet again.

Lassington was known for the venerable oak, thirty feet in girth, which stood for well over 600 years before succumbing in the 1960s. A sapling has now replaced it in Lassington Wood, which is maintained as a nature reserve. In addition, a group of morris dancers based at Highnam has taken Lassington Oak as a name and a logo. Highnam makes its own appearance in Domesday, as *Hamme*, and in another document just fourteen years later (1100) as *Hynehamme*, meaning 'monks' water meadow'. The monks were from St Peter's Abbey, Gloucester; the water meadow was by the River Leadon. There was no church at Highnam in early times. The present building, with spectacular frescoes by Thomas Gambier-Parry, dates from the mid-nineteenth century. Gambier-Parry's son, Hubert Parry, whose monument is in the church (he died in 1918) was a distinguished musician, best known for his setting of 'Jerusalem'.

Over (pronounced *Oover*) in the parish of Highnam was first recorded as *Ofre*, in 804. The word, meaning a slope or bank, referred to the tongue of land between Leadon and Severn. The Romans had a camp here to protect the river crossing; the present A40 roughly follows the line of their road. The Dog Inn dates from when the road was turnpiked in 1726, though it may stand on the site of an earlier building. Its name is explained by two different stories. The first relates that thieves broke in and murdered all the family, save one, who hid in a longcase clock. As the dog stood guard over the clock it was killed by the robbers but they failed to find the person hidden.

The second places the robbery and murders at Ploddy House, near Newent. The robbers' own dog saves the life of the solitary survivor of the household, a maidservant, and in addition leads pursuers to the inn at Over where the criminals are captured as they share out their booty. In deference to the action, the inn changes its name from the Talbot to the Dog. To this day a (somewhat battered) statue of the animal is preserved there. Whatever the merits of such tales criminals were undoubtedly hanged on a gallows set up at Over. One of the last to die in this way was John Davis, aged 58, of Highleadon, executed for sheep stealing in 1789.

The last of the mills on the Leadon was at Over. It existed by c. 1250, when the abbot of Gloucester had to compensate Walter de Musgros, Lord of the Manor of Lassington, for flooding caused on his land as a consequence of the mill's erection. The reason may have been because the Leadon's natural outlet into the Severn was blocked, and its course changed to run south, parallel with that of the Severn. After powering the mill the river passed beneath what is now the A40 and joined the Severn near the present railway bridge. The Gloucester-Hereford canal, cut in the late eighteenth century, started near Westgate Bridge, ran across the Oxleaze, beneath the former Over Causeway (which led to Telford's Bridge), then across part of

Alney Island and under the Maisemore Road (A 417). Boats went into the Severn by means of a lock and crossed to a quay on the far side to rejoin the canal, which continued alongside the Leadon behind Hospital Hillock, a former

*Gates between the Rivers Leadon and (foreground) Severn*

vineyard of St Peter's Abbey (which is still marked on maps).

The Leadon, thus cut off from Over Mill, was re-routed to its present outfall into the Severn, in fact a reversion to the course it had followed in Norman times. The mill was supplied with water from a sluice in the canal, but this arrangement came to an end when a railway superseded the canal. Although auxiliary steam power had been introduced by then, the mill was abandoned in 1885. The last miller, Charles Priday, left to join what became Priday, Metford and Co., whose City Flour Mills at Gloucester Docks closed down only in 1995. The Leadon still flows.

## Walk 14: HIGHNAM, LASSINGTON AND OVER Itinerary

## 5½ miles (2¾ hours), starting at Highnam Post Office (map ref. 794204). with parking in quiet road (Maidenhall).

A. With back to post office, turn left for a few yards, then right along lane with no through road sign. After 200 yards take stile in hedge on left. Follow lefthand hedge through four fields, crossing successive boundaries by gap, stile and double stile. At end of fourth field take stile a few yards to the right of far lefthand corner into strip of woodland (part of Rodwayhill Covert). Go downhill through wood to stile on far side. (In field beyond it would be logical to turn right down slope and then join path re-entering wood to right, but the legal right of way does not lie there). Cross field to far lefthand corner, where bridleway sign stands at roadside (B 4215). At this point, turn about, and re-cross field, roughly following boundary on left. (Beyond this is the track of the former railway, with the River Leadon one field further away). At end of far

*The Lassington Oak*

lefthand salient of field, veer right up bank to hunting gate giving access to wide track through wood. When this passes through gap in hedge follow lefthand edge of field for 250 yards, then re-enter wood and follow path just inside its fringes. At another gap go straight ahead into field and after about 200 yards turn obliquely left to follow track towards tower of Lassington Church (seen below power lines). Follow track to take righthand through farmyard, and pass behind farmhouse, to emerge on lane.

B. Turn right. Pass church on left and pond on right. At brow of gentle rise, turn left through gate by footpath sign. After a few yards, take first stile on left, by a house. Go through a tiny tringular field, over a footbridge and stile, and up a short flight of steps. Go straight across field to stile, then follow path (impeccably cleared bv farmer when we used it) up field to stile in hedge on skyline, keeping roughly parallel with hedge on left. Over stile, go across field towards apex of wood (Lassington Wood). (The Severn Vale appears on the left, with views of Chosen Hill, Gloucester Cathedral and the Cotswold ridge). Take stile into wood (which is maintained as a nature reserve). Of the many paths, choose the one which goes half right down bank. At far end of wood, leave through five-barred gate.

C. Turn left across corner of field and go through narrow gap in hedge to join path between two hedges. When this emerges into field, follow righthand hedge. (River Leadon can be seen on left). Follow what becomes a rough and at times untidy track, usually between hedges. (Where this passes beneath power lines the disused railway bed is immediately adjacent on left; when it starts to go downhill Robinswood Hill is visible ahead). Follow track to emerge on busy A40 dual carriageway by Over Farm Market and the Dog Inn.

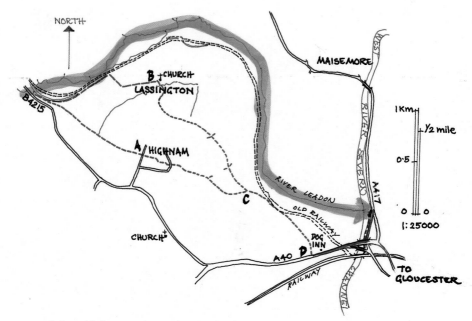

D. Turn left and follow pavement for one third of a mile. Cross west channel of River Severn by road bridge, then turn left along tarmac path. After 150 yards, when path is about to emerge on to side of A417. turn left by Severn Valley Way sign, go down steps, and over stile to river bank. (Almost immediately opposite are the great metal doors which govern the Leadon's entry into the Severn. To the left of them would have been the former canal). Turn left along the river bank and pass beneath the modern road bridge. Beyond it, turn right to cross Telford's bridge. On reaching the A40. turn right for a few yards to reach a path on the right which provides a pedestrian underpass to the other side of the dual carriageway near the disused hospital. Follow the pavement back to Over Farm Market, and turn right (signed Lassington Wood). Retrace steps to point C. There, by five-barred gate, continue on edge of field, with boundary of wood on right. (Spire of Highnam

Church can be seen away to the left). At top of field, swing left to reach road. Go right for some 250 yards. Opposite a 'bus shelter, turn left and follow path between houses with May Hill on horizon ahead. On reaching a road cross to Pipers Grove opposite, then turn right into Limekiln Grove. Follow this to the left, and take asphalt path of only a few yards which leads to playing field. Cross field to gap in hedge to left of house. Take stile to narrow path which runs for 150 yards between hedges/fences to reach lane. Turn left, and after 200 yards return to starting point

**Maps: Pathfinders 1065, *Ross-on-Wye East*, 1066. *Cheltenham*, and 1089, *Gloucester*. Refreshments: Dog Inn, Over (01452 521191).**

# WORKS CONSULTED

| | |
|---|---|
| Andrew Compton | Manuscript notes and photographic slides of the Leadon Valley mills, 1970s (in private hands) |
| Donna Baker | 'An eight-mile ramble where Whittington once walked', *Gloucestershire and Avon Life* (Feb. 1977), 17 |
| A.T.Bannister | *The Place-names of Herefordshire* (privately published, 1916) |
| R.P.Beckinsale | *Companion into Gloucestershire* (1939) |
| Samuel Bentley | *A Short Account of the Church, Episcopal Manor, and other Objects of Interest in Bosbury, Herefordshire* (London and Derby, 1931) |
| Jeff Cooper | 'Lascelles Abercrombie and the Origin of the Poet's Colony at Dymock', *Occasional Papers* 3, Cheltenham and Gloucester College of Higher Education (Cheltenham, 1997) |
| Gwladys M. Davies | 'Mills of the River Leadon and Tributaries', *Newsletter of the Gloucestershire Society for Industrial Archaeology*, no. 7 (Apr. 1966), 26-43 |
| | 'Over Mill', typescript c. 1939 in Gloucestershire Collection, Gloucester City Library |
| Eilert Ekwall | *The Concise Oxford Dictionary of English Place-names* (Oxford, 1991: repr. of 4th ed.) |
| Mary Heane Ellis | 'The Bridges of Gloucester', *Transactions of the Bristol and Gloucestershire Archaeological Society*, 41 (1929), 169-210 |
| T.D.Fosbrooke | *Abstracts of Records and Manuscripts respecting the County of Gloucester, formed into a History* (Gloucester, 1807) |
| Lesley Lee Francis | *The Frost Family's Adventures in Poetry* (Columbia and London, 1994) |
| Robert Frost | *Selected Letters*, ed. Lawrence Thompson (New York, 1965) |
| E. Gethyn-Jones | *Dymock down the Ages* (Dymock, 1985, 2nd ed.) |
| | 'Roman Dymock - A Personal Record', *Transactions of the Bristol and Gloucestershire Archaeological Society*, 109 (1991), 91-98 |
| | *A Short History of the Parish and Church of Donnington* (Dymock, 1958) |
| Gloucestershire Federation of Women's Institutes | |
| | *Gloucestershire within Living Memory* (Newbury and Gloucester, 1996) |
| Richard B. Grantham | *Drainage of the Leadon Valley* (1868) |
| Irvine Gray and J.E. Gethyn Jones | |
| | *The Registers of the Church of St Mary, Dymock, 1538-1790* (Bristol, 1960) |
| G.B.Grundy | *Saxon Charters of Worcestershire* (Birmingham, 1931) |
| Ivor Gurney | *Collected Poems*, ed. P.J.Kavanagh (Oxford, 1984) |
| R.H. | 'Notes on Maisemore', manuscript of c. 1871 in Gloucestershire Collection, Gloucester City Library |
| J.W.Haines | 'The Dymock Poets', *Gloucestershire Countryside*, 1 (1931-4), 131-3 |
| | 'The Flora of Gloucestershire', *ibid.*, 105-6 |
| | *In Memoriam: Edward Thomas as I Knew Him* (1919) |
| | 'The Leadon Country', *Gloucestershire Countryside*, 1 (1931-4), 20 |
| | 'Mr Robert Frost. An American Poet in Gloucestershire', *Gloucestershire Journal* (2 Feb. 1935). 20 |
| Linda Hart | *Once They Lived in Gloucestershire. A Dymock Poets Anthology* (Lechlade, |

|                              | 1995)                                                                                                              |
| Joe Hillaby                  | *Ledbury, a Medieval Borough* (Almeley and Ledbury, 1997; orig.publ. as *The Book of Ledbury*, 1982)               |
| Della Hooke                  | *The Anglo-Saxon Landscape. The Kingdom of the Hwicce* (Manchester, 1985)                                          |
|                              | *Worcestershire Anglo-Saxon Charter-bounds* (Ipswich, 1990)                                                        |
| Maurice A. Lulham            | *The Wye Valley Otter Hounds, 1874-1935* (Cheltenham, 1936)                                                        |
| Edna Lyall (Ada Ellen Bayly) |                                                                                                                    |
|                              | *In Spite of All* (1901)                                                                                           |
| H. J. Massingham             | *Shepherd's Country* (1938)                                                                                        |
| John Masefield               | *Grace before Ploughing. Fragments of Autobiography* (1966)                                                        |
|                              | *The Ledbury Scene* (Hereford, nd; orig. 1951)                                                                     |
|                              | *So Long to Learn. Chapters of an Autobiography* (1952)                                                            |
| Stephen Mills and Pierce Riemer |                                                                                                                 |
|                              | *The Mills of Gloucestershire* (1989)                                                                             |
| Travers Morgan               | *Changing River Landscapes* (Cheltenham, 1987)                                                                     |
| National Rivers Authority    |                                                                                                                    |
|                              | *River Severn Lower Reaches Catchment Management Plan Consultation Report* (Tewkesbury, 1995)                      |
| Roy Palmer                   | *The Folklore of Gloucestershire* (Tiverton, 1994)                                                                |
|                              | *The Folklore of Hereford and Worcester* (Almeley, 1992)                                                          |
| Nikolaus Pevsner             | *The Buildings of England: Herefordshire* (Harmondsworth, 1963)                                                   |
| Charles J. Robinson          | *A History of the Mansions and Manors of Herefordshire* (London and Hereford, 1872)                               |
| A.H. Smith                   | *The Place-names of Gloucestershire*, 4 vols (Cambridge, 1964-5)                                                  |
| Seán Street                  | *The Dymock Poets* (Bridgend, 1994)                                                                               |
| David Verey                  | *The Buildings of England. Gloucestershire: The Cotswolds* (Harmondsworth, 1986)                                 |
|                              | *The Buildings of England. Gloucestershire: The Vale and the Forest of Dean* (1988)                              |
| A.R. Winnington-Ingram       |                                                                                                                    |
|                              | 'On the Origin of Names of Places with Special Reference to Gloucestershire', *Proceedings of the Cotteswold Naturalists' Field Club*, 9 (1895), 21-39 |
| Geoffrey N. Wright           | 'The Quiet Vale of Leadon', *Country Life* (19 Jul.1973), 142-4                                                   |

# Index

## A

Abbot's Place  56
Abercrombie, Catherine  36
Abercrombie, Lascelles  29, 35, 36, 41
Abertillery, hop pickers from  21
Acton Beauchamp  6, 13
Acton Cross  13, 14
Addison, Joseph  28
Alney Island  65
Ann Cam School  36
Ashleworth  40

## B

Bar Lane  60
Barber's Bridge  56, 57, 58
Barrett Browning Memorial Institute,
    Ledbury  25, 32
Barrett, Elizabeth  25
Beacon Hill  16, 18
Beckinsale, R.P.  28
Black Harry, gypsy king  21
Blackwells End  56
Bloody Verlands  13
Blount, Thomas  24
Bosbury  6, 13, 16, 20, 22
Bromsberrow  12
Bromyard Downs  12
Brooke, Rupert  36
Brooms Green  38
Butters End  56
Bye Street, Ledbury  25
Byett, James  64

## C

Canning Family  61

Canon Frome  13
Catley Brook  18
Catley Cross  16
Church Lane, Ledbury  24
Churches
    Bosbury  20
    Dymock  32, 36, 37, 38
    Kempley  32
    Ledbury  30
    Maisemore  61, 62
    Rudford  57, 58
    St Andrew, Evesbatch  13, 14
    St John, Pauntley  45, 46
    St Katherine's Chapel, Ledbury  24
    St Mary, Hartpury  56, 59, 63
    Upleadon  49, 50, 51, 54
City Flour Mills, Gloucester Docks  65
Civil War  13, 20, 25, 57
Coddington Brook  22
Collier's Bridge  16, 18
Collinpark Wood  45, 49
Congreve, William  28
Cormeilles, Ansfrid de  45
Corse  50
Corse End  56
Cotswolds  7, 29, 62

## D

d'Abitot Family  44
Daffodil Fields, The, poem  29
daffodils  28, 29, 36, 44
Davies, Gwladys M.  53
Davies, W.H.  36
Davis, John  65
de Lacy, Walter  48
Dick Whittington  45
Dobyns, Margaret, monument  13
Domesday Book  6, 12, 28, 33, 57, 64
Donnington  28
Drinkwater, John  36
Dryden, John  28

Dudley, hop pickers from  21
Durbridge 41,  44
Dymock 6,  7,  29,  36,  38,  40,  42
Dymock Poets 6,  28,  32,  36

## E

Eastnor  48
Eden's Hill  49
Edgar, King  6
Ekwall, Eilert  24,  37
Ell Brook  6,  52,  54
Ellis, George  40
England's Bridge  16,  18,  23
*Everlasting Mercy, The*, poem  25
Evesbatch  12,  13,  14,  16
Evesbatch Court  14

## F

Farjeon, Eleanor  29
Feast of St Giles  61
Flaxley Abbey  37
Fosbrooke, T.D.  45
Fromes Hill  16
Frost, Robert  7,  29,  35,  36,  44

## G

Gambier-Parry, Thomas  64
Gethyn-Jones, Eric  32,  37
Gibson, Wilfrid  29,  35,  36
Gladstone, William  20
Gloucester  7,  12
   See of  6
Gloucester-Hereford canal  21,  25,  65
Gloucestershire Home for Wayfarers  45
Gloucestershire Wildlife Trust  42,  49
Glyn Iddens  29
Glynch Brook  6,  48,  50
Gorsley Wood  52
Great Malvern  6
Greenway  28,  30,  36

Gurney, Ivor  6,  60
Guy Fawkes  52

## H

Haines, John  7,  29,  35,  36,  44,  64
Hall House Meadows  29
Halmonds Frome  12,  14
Harford Family  20
Harold, King  28
Hartpury  56,  57,  58,  60,  61,  62
Hartpury Agricultural College  61
Hartpury Court  56,  63
Hartpury House  61
Harvey, W.H.  76
Hasards Bank  32
Hasards Quarry  32
Hayward, John  24
Herdman-Smith, Robert  44
Hereford  21
   Bishops of  20,  28
   Diocese  6
Hereford and Worcester Canal  33
Herefordshire Record Office  28
High Street, Ledbury  24
Highleadon 8,  60,  65
Highnam  66
Highnam Wood  61
Homend, Ledbury  24
Hooper, Joseph and Robert  37
Hope End  25
Hope, William  37
Hospital Hillock  65
Hunting Bridge  61
Huntsman's Bridge  44,  46
Hwicce: people  6

# I

*In Spite of All*, novel  20
Inns
    Beauchamp Arms, Dymock  39, 43
    Bell Inn, Bosbury  22, 23
    Canning Arms, Hartpury  51
    Dog Inn, Over  64, 67
    Feathers Hotel, Ledbury  24, 27
    Full Pitcher, Ledbury  27, 31
    Horseshoe, Brooms Green  30, 31, 39
    Majors Arms, Evesbatch  14
    Majors Arms, Halmonds Frome  15
    Oak, Staplow  23
    Rising Sun, Hartpury  63
    Rose and Crown, Redmarley  47
    Royal Exchange, Hartpury  51
    Seven Stars, Ledbury  25, 27
    Swan, Staunton  51
    Talbot Hotel, Ledbury  24, 27
    Watersmeet, Hartpury  51
    Wheatsheaf, Fromes Hill  19
    White Hart, Maisemore  63

# J

John Masefield Way  32

# K

Kempley Brook  6, 37
Ketford  45, 46
Ketford Bridge  40, 42, 44
Kilcot Wood  52
Knapp, The  25

# L

Lassington  61, 64, 66
Lassington Oak  64
Lassington Wood  61, 64
Leachford Brook  53
Leadington  7, 28, 29, 34, 36
Leadon, River

catchment area  6
flooding  7, 21, 44
flora of  7, 28, 36, 44, 53
Leadon Valley  7, 28, 29, 32, 52
Ledbury
    6, 7, 21, 24, 26, 28, 30, 32, 60
battle of  24
Ledbury Park  24
Leominster  24
Limbury Hill  52
Little Iddens  29, 36
Lyall, Edna  20

# M

Magonsaetan - people  6
Maisemore  60, 61, 62, 64
Malvern Hills  12, 14, 16, 42, 55
Marcle Ridge  38, 42
Market Hall, Ledbury  25
Market House, Ledbury  24, 25
Masefield, John
    6, 7, 24, 25, 26, 29, 30, 45
Massey, Colonel  24
Massingham, H.J.  56
Mathon  16
May Hill  7, 16, 29, 39, 50, 52
Mills
    Bosbury Upper Mill  16
    Brass Mill  52
    Cleeve Mill  52
    Crookes Mill  52
    Cut Mill  6
    Dodd's Mill  16, 18
    Durbridge Mill  44
    Farm Mill  37
    Fawkes's Mill  52
    Forge Mill  49
    Harridge Mill  44
    Hartpury Mill  52, 56
    Hazle Mill  33
    Highleadon Mill  56

Ketford Mill 40, 42
Leather Mill 33
Malswick Mill 52, 53, 54
New Mills, Ledbury 25
Okle Pitcher Mill 52
Over Mill 65
Pauntley Mill 45
Payford Mill 44, 46
Rudford Mill 57
Stocks Mill 44, 46
Upleadon Mill 6, 48, 49
Milton, John 28
Monks' Bridge 37, 38
Moor End 56
Moore, John 21
Morgan
Travers 7
Murrells End 56
Musgros, Walter de 65

## N

New House 24
New Street, Ledbury 25
Newent 25, 45, 52, 60, 65

## O

Okle Green 55
Old Gloucester Road 60
Old Grammar School, Ledbury 24
Old Grange, Dymock 37
Old Nail Shop, Greenway 29, 30
Oldfields 29
Over 7, 64, 66
Over Causeway 65
Oxenhall 52

## P

Parry, Hubert 64
Parry, Mr. Jack 21
Pauncefoot family 28
Pauntley 8, 45, 46

Pauntley Court 45, 46
Payford Bridge 45, 46
Pershore Abbey 6
Pevsner, Nikolaus 24, 25
Pie's Nest 29, 30
Ploddy House 65
Poets' Paths 29, 38
Pollet, Monsieur V. 45
Pope, Alexander 28
Preston Brook 6, 37
Price, W.P. 57
Priday, Charles 65
Priday, Metford and Co. 65
Prior's Court 21

## R

Railway lines
    Gloucester to Ledbury 25, 33
    Hereford to Worcester 25
Red Brook 57
Red Hill 52
Redmarley d'Abitot 6, 7, 44
Romans 6, 36, 37, 40, 60, 61, 64
Rudford 57, 58
Rupert, Prince 20, 24
Ruskin, John 20
Ryton 36
Ryton Firs 41

## S

*September Moon*, novel 21
Severn, River 6, 7, 37, 40, 57, 64, 65
Shropshire Hills 12
Skynner, Edward 24
Southend, Ledbury 24
Spring Hill 60
St Peter's Abbey 48, 56, 64, 65
Staplow 21, 22
Staunton 50
Steen's Brook 16
Stony Brook 22

## T

Taylor, Hannah  57
Taylor, Isaac  45
Telford's Bridge, Gloucester  65
Tewkesbury  21
Thackwell, John  37
Thomas, Edward  7,  29,  35,  36
Tibberton  58
Tibberton Brook  6,  58
Tonson, Jacob  28

## U

Upleadon  48,  50,  52
Upleadon Court  48,  50,  51

## W

Wall Hills  24
Walwyn family  28
Ward Hill  13
Wellington Court  21
Westgate Bridge  65
Whitmore, John  50
Whittington Family  45
*Widow in the Bye Street, The*, poem  25
William the Conqueror  12,  48
Wilton Place  37
Windcross  37
Winnington-Ingram, Rev.A.R.  61
Witlaf, King of Mercia  20
Woodruff, Wilford  16
Worcester Diocese  6
Wye, River  37
Wye Valley Otter Hunt  21,  41

High Lassington I see your woods again
Blown all about with wet and falling rain,
What Druid spell have you cast over me
Sweet woodlands of my dear, my own country.

*W.H. Harvey*